'Speaking on similar themes to Rob Frost's excellent book, an excited minister confronted me: "That was terrific! I am going back to haul my church into the twentieth century." "You had better hurry," I replied. "You've got less than four years to do it!" This is a book for twenty-first century Christianity. The pain of change will be significant. But without it we will become irrelevant.'

GERALD COATES
Team Leader, Pioneer

'Rob Frost has drawn on his wide experience of working with the institutional church and his book will resonate with all those longing for a new reformation of the church. The book is rooted in the reality of where we are, but it offers a cluster of visions for the way ahead. Certainly a book to assist leaders and churches to prepare for the mission challenges of the twenty-first century.'

DAVID COFFEY
Secretary, Baptist Union

'This is a mega-motivating, cutting edge heartcry for reality in the church and in our own lives.'

GEORGE VERWER
International Director, Operation Mobilisation

'A classic, much needed radical recall to a kingdom-centred future church of small, dispersed, action congregations.'

JOHN VINCENT
Former President of Methodist Conference

'A blunt, uncompromising view of things as they are – with a radical, prophetic call outlining how things could be in the future. We ignore Rob Frost's analysis at our peril. Essential reading.'

RUSS BRAVO
Editor, New Christian Herald

'Dr Frost has in his own ministry fearlessly faced the challenges taking place in the world's cultures, and sought to respond to them in gospel-based and relevant ways with considerable success. The passionate seriousness of his challenge in this book needs to be pondered by all who take Christian mission seriously.'

DONALD ENGLISH

'What will the church of the future be like? Drawing on four years of research, Dr Rob Frost foresees a church of many small communities with visionary leaders – "a church of many welcomes". I like that!'

PATRICK HARRIS
Bishop of Southwell

'That the church needs to radically reassess how it achieves its primary task – fulfilling the great commission – is painfully obvious. Declining numbers, organisational and financial difficulties, even uncertainty about core beliefs, have led to a sense of crisis among Christians. Rob Frost helps us to face these issues. This is a book to be read and debated, argued with and acted on. It is not the final word on charting the way forward, but it is a stimulating and provocative prod in the right direction.'

SIMON JONES
Editor, Christianity Magazine

'A book to get under the skin of church leaders. It will get readers debating the way ahead for mission-minded churches.'

GEOFFREY ROPER
General Secretary, Free Church Federal Council

'The sort of dynamite that will break through the thickets to allow the new life that God's Spirit is building today to survive into the next generation. A must for all who care for God's church.'

'This is a damning critique of the present state of the mainline church, which has significance beyond Methodism. Sadly, its picture of a paralysed church and mistaken agendas is all too recognisable. Thankfully, it does not seek merely to knock down, but to build up, and it points the way forward for the church to get over its current impasse. Rob's solutions are radical – and rightly so. Every church leader should be asked to respond to this book.'

'There is only one way for the church – forwards. Rob's look backwards is only to envision us more intensely for the future. The best is yet to be.'

'Dr Frost raises issues that we need to face urgently.'

Also by Rob Frost:

Methods of Mission (C) (Methodist Publishing House, 1979)
Big Questions (Bible Society, 1983)
Conversation Starters (Bible Society, 1983)
Break Me, Shape Me (Marshall Pickering, 1986)
Go for Growth (Bible Society, 1986)
Visions (Moorley's, 1986)
Breaking Bread (Kingsway, 1988)
People at Work (Pergamon Educational Productions, 1988)
Pilgrims (Kingsway, 1990)
Gospel End (Monarch, 1991)
Broken Cross (Monarch, 1992)
Burning Questions (Monarch, 1994)
When I Can't Pray (Kingsway, 1995)
Thinking Clearly About God and Science (with David Wilkinson) (Monarch, 1996)
For Such a Time as This (C) (Scripture Union, 1996)

(C) = Contributor

Which Way for the Church?

ROB FROST

KINGSWAY PUBLICATIONS
EASTBOURNE

First published 1997

ISBN 0 85476 717 7

Designed and produced by Bookprint Creative Services
P.O. Box 827, BN21 3YJ, England for
KINGSWAY PUBLICATIONS LTD
Lottbridge Drove, Eastbourne, East Sussex BN23 6NT.
Printed in Great Britain.

Dedicated to my father, Ronald,
with thanks for his constant encouragement and ongoing vision;
to my sons, Andy and Chris,
with thanks for keeping me in touch with the emerging generation;
and to all the 'Easter People',
with thanks for sharing the vision.

Contents

Foreword

The church of Jesus Christ has a past – often glorious, but in some periods an embarrassment for us to recall. Such times were often prompted by a reluctance to ask questions, and a bland acceptance of the concept that the traditions of yesterday should always apply to the church of tomorrow.

It is my conviction that for the church to be truly relevant to contemporary society, and in line with the purposes of God rather than the will of humankind, we must be prepared to allow the living God to disturb our comfort zones, and confront those difficult questions which will challenge our complacency.

Rob Frost is therefore a brave man. For he has been prepared to both challenge and confront the church of today with the implications of what our future in God could be like. This provides disturbing reading, for it is human tradition rather than divine truth which is rejected in this book. Rob makes us ask what shape the church of the future should be, and how we should live if we are to act as a church which radically challenges society with the reality of a biblical gospel worked out in our daily lives. While not all may agree with every conclusion Rob draws, this book offers uncomfortable reading for the self-satisfied, but a salutary reminder that God requires a church for tomorrow which responds to divine direction rather than a comfortable acquiescence to the contemporary status quo.

CLIVE CALVER
Director General, Evangelical Alliance

Acknowledgements

With sincere thanks to Dr Peter Clarke and the staff and post-grad students of King's College, London (1991–5) who moved me out of my comfort zone with their stimulating discussion and hard questions. I am also greatly indebted to Luiz Montanhero and the staff of Ashton University Business School.

Thanks to my friends Stuart and Leny Cato and Fran and Piers Lane, and my wife, Jacqui, who helped me to start my writing during lazy days in France. To Meryl Smith for her ability to unhang my computer and explain the most complex computer operations in words of one syllable, and to Jacky Barker, for help with the Bibliography. (Special thanks to *Windows '95*!)

Thanks to the line managers of Easter People for hearing my ideas, and to Matt Bird for allowing reference to his thesis, 'Is Church Growth the Result of Methodology or the Work of God?' Thanks to Judith Rossall, Paul Smith, Peter Stephens, Lee Proudlove and Piers Lane for helpful suggestions for the discussion sections.

Introduction

I love the church, and have a special affection for the Methodist denomination in which I was reared. Within this fellowship I found my faith, and I am thankful to God for the wonderful context it has provided for ministry.

This book is not written in order to tear down and destroy the church in general or Methodism in particular. It comes out of a strong desire to create and to build. My prayer is that the ideas it conveys will facilitate discussion, stimulate vision and promote new strategies for the church of the new millennium.

I am not disheartened about the state of the church, as many are, for I see a great and wonderful future. I hope that what I have written will help many to dream a new dream of what the church may become, and will give strength to those who are losing hope.

Much of the thinking was done during my four years of part-time research at King's College, London, as I wrote my PhD. As I read around my subject and explored British demography, social history, the evolution of culture, contemporary management theory and church-planting strategy I began to form strong views about contemporary church life.

This book, then, is not my PhD thesis, but it does flow from serious research in an academic environment. I have no doubt that it will offend some, anger others and may even lose me some good friends! Nevertheless, I needed to write it, and I hope that it will make us all think again about what the church is, and what it might become.

Rob Frost
London, April 1997

CHAPTER 1

A Vision for Change

The preservation society

Preservation is part of the British way of life, and our urge to preserve is expressed in countless peculiar ways. Some people invest inordinate amounts of time in preserving old steam trains. They dismantle them, reassemble them, polish them and display them. Occasionally they may even coax them to puff and pant their way up the line to obscurity.

For others, the urge to preserve may be focused on vintage cars, decrepit buses, traction engines, steamrollers or ancient harvesting machines. For many, however, this rather quaint characteristic of the British finds expression in something much more dangerous. They are driven by a need to preserve the church.

This preservation society is not just concerned with sanctuaries, spires, graveyards and pews; it has a tenacious hold on much of contemporary church life. It strangles new initiatives, suppresses creativity and smothers anything which threatens to disturb the safety of the familiar.

This is the society which holds on to worn-out liturgies, protects meaningless traditions, catalogues past triumphs, conserves chapel culture and polishes the pews. It preserves the work of God in a glass case where it can disturb no one.

When I first entered the musty library of my theological college I discovered that a worn-out left boot was prominently displayed in a dusty glass case. A neatly written label described it as belonging to the famous Primitive Methodist revivalist Hugh Bourne. I often wondered what the college authorities would have done if he had returned from glory to collect it! I could not credit that either he, or his simple firebrand gospel, would have been welcome in the liberal context of that cloistered community.

The members of the preservation society prefer the kingdom of God to be housed in a museum; the church embalmed in lifeless institutionalism; the people of God stored safely as dry bones. Sadly, while they are labouring to preserve the life of the church, they actually hasten its death.

This is one preservation society which urgently needs to be disbanded. Its devotees are found in the leadership of many mainline church denominations and they cannot glimpse the kingdom of God for the traditions of men. They do not know what God is doing, but focus on what he has done. They can't see the future for the past. The church of tomorrow is thwarted by the preservation society because it treats new life as a threat. Pioneers are condemned, revolutionaries are despised and prophets are ignored. Sadly, the members of the preservation society hold tight to the reins of power in the institutional church.

Before we can look forward it's good to look back and, if possible, learn from the mistakes of those who have gone before. The story of the eighteenth-century revival and the growth of early Methodism illustrates how the preservation society went about its business. It was mobilised into fervent activity when new life threatened the stability of eighteenth-century institutional Christianity.

The struggle between Wesley and the established church of the eighteenth century is a prime example of a struggle between a pioneer and a preservation society; between a revolutionary and an establishment; between a prophet and an institution; between powerlessness and power. It makes a good case study for examining the conflict between preservation and vision, and sets the context for the message of this book, which is a message about change.

A life-changing theology

Anglican Christianity in the eighteenth century wasn't much more than a sedate religious ethic. It was deeply affected by the growth of a popular form of deism among the intellectuals of the time. John Tillotson (1630–94) and Thomas Tenison (1636–1715), two of its leading proponents, both became Archbishops of Canterbury. They taught that reason could provide all that was needed for divine truth. There was a declining emphasis on biblical doctrine and an increasing reliance on 'the truths of natural religion'.

The way was open, even in the highest circles of the Church of England, for the belief that revelation must give way to reason. A cold mist of doubt hung over specifically Christian doctrines for more than half a century, and most preachers preferred to proclaim the acceptable gospel of 'morality'. The theological climate was exceedingly bleak.

Lots of people from different social backgrounds came to believe that Christianity was false and dropped all religious observance. The majority, however, believed that the Church of England was a necessary support for the monarchy and a key factor in the maintenance of peace, and so asserted that traditional religious practice should be maintained.

The preservation society lacked the power of a living faith and settled for maintaining a comfortable institution which kept it safe. This church certainly wouldn't change the world, but it might help to preserve it!

The eighteenth-century preservation society was united in its suspicion of 'enthusiasm'. The term meant much the same as 'fanatic' today, and they applied it to anyone whose practice of Christianity manifested any fervour. Such religion was considered to be a threat to the peace of the realm. They preferred religion to be quietly dispassionate.

John Wesley's theology respected the authority of the Bible. He opposed the domination of reason which his Anglican contemporaries so appreciated, and he defied the reliance on 'feelings' which was strongly advocated by revivalists. Wesley chose a middle way – an awesome respect for the Bible, interpreted in the light of reason, church tradition and personal experience. His evangelistic fervour and his advocacy of 'the strangely warmed heart' challenged the cold deism of the established church, but he fiercely protected his followers from the fanaticism which England had seen in the previous century. The thousands of industrial workers who gathered at Wesley's 'field meetings' were looking for a different message from the one proclaimed in their local parish church. They were seeking a Christian experience which gave them a sense of identity, self-worth and meaning at a time of enormous social upheaval.

Wesley's message was not about preserving an institution, protecting a way of life or maintaining a social order. It was a message of repentance, of forgiveness and of a living relationship with God. It challenged the cold reason of the preservation society with its lack of power and personal experience.

Popular preaching

It is little wonder that the power-brokers of the established church's preservation society did their utmost to exclude Wesley from their hallowed institution. They managed to keep him out of most of the pulpits in the land and he was forced to preach in the open air.

The necessity of preaching outside in the open air turned out to be the 'shop window' of the new Methodist movement. The activity was first popularised by George Whitefield. Gillie described one of Whitefield's early London meetings in his Journal:

> Public notice having been given... upon coming out of the coach he found an incredible number of people assembled. Many had told him that he should never come again out of that place alive. He went in, however, between two of his friends, who, by the pressure of the crowd were soon parted entirely from him and were obliged to leave him at the mercy of the rabble. But these, instead of hurting him, formed a lane for him and carried him along to the middle of the fields... from whence he preached without molestation to an exceedingly great multitude.

The meetings grew more and more popular until tens of thousands were gathering night after night to hear the preaching of this twenty-four-year-old parson. Later, the meetings were held in Kennington to provide more space, and on Sunday 6th May 1739 Whitefield wrote in his diary:

> At six preached at Kennington. Such a sight I never saw before. I believe there were no less than fifty thousand people, and near four score coaches, besides great numbers of horses... God gave me great enlargement of heart. I continued my discourse for an hour and a half, and when I returned, I was filled with such love, peace and joy that I cannot express it.

On 2nd April 1739 Wesley took over Whitefield's field-preaching work, and it was to become the hallmark of his ministry: 'At four in the afternoon I submitted to be more vile, and proclaimed in the highways the glad tidings of salvation, speaking from a little eminence in ground adjoining the city to about three thousand people.'

Like Whitefield, Wesley was deeply moved by the prospect which such a ministry opened up. It gave him the opportunity to reach vast numbers of people in various parts of the country, and provided a national platform from which he could expound his message of salvation for all. He was no longer confined to small religious societies, but had an audience numbering tens of thousands.

The field preachers of the eighteenth century were effective in reaching a secularised and unchurched culture. They were able to speak in ways that the working class found exciting and dramatic. Little wonder, then, that the preservation society of the day found their preaching coarse and distasteful. Had they not shut their pulpits to Wesley, he may never have discovered how to reach the poor and the powerless who heard him in the fields.

Cultural relevance

The culture of the established churches alienated the new industrial workers of the woollen, cotton and iron boom-towns. This alienation was epitomised by the 'pew system' which enabled the wealthy to purchase and furnish their own areas of a church. Many of the pews were built with tall partitions so that the affluent could worship in complete privacy. Sometimes they were curtained, sometimes filled with sofas and tables, or even provided with fireplaces. It was not uncommon for a servant to enter between the prayers and the sermon with sherry and light refreshments.

The poor, meanwhile, were restricted to the coldest and darkest parts of the church where it was difficult to see or hear anything. This traffic in pews excluded the poor and symbolised the church's attitude towards them.

The preservation society in eighteenth-century Anglicanism was made up of powerful members of the establishment. They had little time for the emerging working-class culture of the newly industrialised towns, and were happy to retain a form of church life which shut them out. The enthusiasm of the early Methodist converts was regarded with great suspicion by the preservation society, and many associated them with the kind of stereotypes attributed to new movements. Early Methodists were accused of kidnapping children, encouraging sexual licence, disrupting family ties and practising sorcery.

Stevenson noted:

> The antagonism to Methodism was most prevalent during its initial impact on an area, when still an unknown quantity, and rumours about behaviour were most likely to be given credence. In general terms the opposition to the Methodists began to slacken from the middle of the century but it could still flare up when they evangelised new areas; for example disturbances recurred in Cornwall towards the end of the century when the Methodists moved into the eastern part of the county.

As the Methodist movement grew more acceptable, and its members became respected members of the community, the church developed an association with the Trade Union movement. They soon emerged as leaders, for the Methodist members tended to stay sober, obey the law and help one another. Methodists had the courage to stand up to fellow-workers and employers, and were willing to give time to meetings and organisation. Their preaching gave them experience of public speaking, which was useful in political life. A study of local union leaders in East Anglia showed that 95 per cent of all those whose religion was known were Methodists. The powerful leaders of the established church did not approve of this kind of affiliation.

Wesley's movement began out of doors and outside of religious buildings, and this made it approachable to the unchurched communities of the new towns. The popular style of proclamation made its message understandable to uneducated working-class communities. The Methodist commitment to improving working-class living standards through trade unionism also won them respect and popularity. Unlike the established church, this was a church which was in touch with the working-class people of the new industrial towns.

The preservation society served the power-brokers of this world and it had no time for the godless poor. It saw Wesley's movement as a threat because it was not in league with the landowner, the squire, the industrialist and the politician. Wesley's movement was in touch with the poor, the powerless and the newly emerging working classes. It was a religion of the people.

Dynamic leadership

Wesley was able to raise working-class members to exalted positions of leadership in his societies and to exercise energetic pastoral care among his members through an army of 8,000 class leaders and 700 preachers.

Wesley's preachers exercised a radically different style of leadership from that of the established church. In many communities the parson was dependent on the squire – a dependence which was often an economic, social and cultural alliance. The role of the parson was to care for the rich and powerful rather than the weak and oppressed.

Rarely can a national church have been so lacking in leadership and cohesion. The chief cause of the chaos was the failure of the Houses of Convocation to meet regularly, and when they did assemble it was to no creative purpose. When Convocation was called following the Act of Toleration of 1689, its sessions were marked by the most acrimonious wrangling between the majority of the bishops in the Upper House and the majority of the inferior clergy in the Lower. Most bishops did what they wanted in their own diocese. Many of them spent two-thirds of the year in London because they dare not miss voting time at the House of Lords. Their absence would be noted, and would prevent them from rising to the higher echelons of church life. Some bishops rarely visited their diocese at all. Confirmations, when they did take place, involved vast numbers of people all at once.

Members of the preservation society were more concerned with keeping their own positions in the power structure than with the social revolution which was happening before their very eyes. By contrast, the leaders of the Methodist movement were battle-weary heroes, willing to suffer for the faith they proclaimed and who earned respect among the working classes for their courage and daring.

Nelson, Maxfield and other itinerant preachers were carried off by army press gangs. Thomas Mitchell was thrown repeatedly into a deep pond until he was unconscious and then his clothes were covered with paint. William Seward was blinded by one Welsh mob and killed by another. Several others were killed or maimed, or they burned themselves out with exhaustion. Thomas Olivers travelled a hundred thousand miles on one horse.

These preachers did not live a life of idle luxury or strut the London political scene. They rose every morning at four and preached most mornings at five. They abstained from liquor and usually divided the day into eight hours for sleeping and eating, eight for study and meditation, and eight for preaching, visitation and social concern.

After the imprisonment of one of his preachers, Wesley wrote: 'I pray you for what pay could we procure men to do this service? To be always ready to go to prison or to death?'

The established church could not raise a leadership to match the commitment and enthusiasm of Wesley's preachers. The members of the preservation society were too concerned with tradition, security and safety to risk their lives for the kingdom of God. They were too satisfied with the fading glory of human acclaim to suffer for the eternal glory of the kingdom of heaven.

Prime locations

The preservationists in the established church were unable to respond to the massive demographic shift resulting from the industrial revolution. Preservation societies are not good at high-risk activity which looks at what will be, rather than what has been. Hence the established church continued to put its resources into traditional agricultural areas in the south, where the most effective Anglican parishes of the 'closed' style went on much as before. The squire was still dominant and held the sanctions of social control. As a result, the southern counties, except for Cornwall, Devon and Middlesex, continued to be a 'Methodist desert' well into the nineteenth century.

The Anglicans were weak and ineffective in the newly industrialised areas, however, and generally remained so until the reforming legislation under Peel. The flexible organisation of Methodism meant that Wesley's preachers could provide religious services for thousands of people not reached by the Church of England. Wickham observed in *Church and People in an Industrial City*: 'Where the national church required an Act of Parliament, a grant of money, an educated gentleman and a crop of lawyers, the Methodists required only a friendly barn and a zealous preacher – at least for a beginning.'

The parish system was a legacy of medieval law. New parishes could not be created without a private Act of Parliament, and this was a cumbersome procedure; besides, local vested interests looked askance at parish boundary changes. In the newly industrialised areas the institutional church hardly touched the population at all.

The patterns of settlement in the Shropshire coalfield created great difficulties for the territorial parish. Trinder's book *The Industrial Revolution in Shropshire* noted: 'Mining and iron-making villages grew up with complete disregard for established ecclesiastical boundaries and remote from parish churches.' In this area, non-residence, pluralism and clerical poverty exacerbated the church's problems.

Throughout the expanding industrial towns of the North and the Black Country the Church of England's parochial machinery was totally inadequate. The Anglican preservation society was too intent on maintaining its hold over the idyllic villages of traditional England to bother with these emerging new towns of the industrial revolution. The whole system was geared to sustaining the past rather than to responding to its rapidly changing social context.

In 1815 the Province of York, with its burgeoning new towns, had only 2,000 parishes compared with 10,000 in the Province of Canterbury. In Manchester there were still only fifty-six churches when the population had grown to 515,581. In Liverpool the total church accommodation amounted to about 21,000 seats for a population of 94,000.

In the woollen towns the picture was much the same. In Bradford between 1800 and 1840 only three Anglican churches were built as the population boomed from 13,264 to 66,715. It is little wonder, therefore, that in 1851 Bradford had the third-highest proportion of Nonconformists in the urban areas of England.

In 1837 the Vicar of Leeds was still pastorally responsible for a population of some 125,000 people, with a chapelry system which had proved unworkable even in the eighteenth century. Wearmouth concluded: 'There is little doubt that Methodism owed its early and substantial success in Leeds to the weakness of the Anglican chapelry system and the lack of Anglican churches in the rapidly growing areas of the town.'

Methodism grew in the gaps of the parish system. Methodist circuits with over a thousand members at the end of the eighteenth century were generally found in the grossly under-churched industrial towns, of which Leeds, Bradford and Halifax were good examples. The established church's inability to respond to new opportunities in new towns gave the early Methodists a window of opportunity for mission and growth. Humphreys wrote:

In effect Methodism became a form of Dissent, casting its spell on thousands whom the Church did not touch, and the greatest religious movement of the time fell largely outside the Establishment. Churchmen and Dissenters had every excuse for suspicion; convulsions and apocalyptic frenzies seized the early congregations as if with a consuming fire. Yet there was hardly any other channel for the sense that Methodism brought – that of the soul's condition.

The preservation society so active in eighteenth-century Anglicanism tried to preserve the church from the raw dynamic of a living faith. It looked with disdain on forms of evangelism such as field preaching. It wooed the power-brokers of the day, but ignored the poor of the industrial towns. It refused to move resources to serve the newly emerging industrial towns. It employed a 'professional' clergy who could not communicate with the impoverished masses, and it appointed bishops whose work demonstrated self-interest rather than self-sacrifice. The preservation society maintained an order of church life which should have been thrown out long ago.

Dynamic vision

The preservation society is still active today. Its members in the mainline denominations hinder mission and stop the church from becoming culturally relevant. History is repeating itself, but with the Methodist Church in the role of the established church, and the new radical house church as the effective growing movement.

There has been a dramatic decline within the Methodist Church between 1970 and 1990. During the same period, however, the seeds of a new church movement in Britain were beginning to take root. Figures produced by Marc Europe (a Christian research agency) revealed that the new house-church movement grew by 78 per cent between 1969 and 1979. The figures from the survey 'Christian England' indicate a growth of 144 per cent in this group between 1979 and 1989, with membership rising from 44,400 in 1979 to 108,500 in 1989. The survey indicated that 1,000 members per week were being lost jointly by the Anglican, Catholic and Methodist denominations over the same period.

Dr David Harper of the Hallam University Business School looked at the growth of the 'new' churches from a business perspective in a paper entitled 'Going for growth in a Christian setting'.

> There has been some very significant growth amongst the so called 'new churches' (formerly known as house churches). The new churches currently have 140,000 members (viz 1994). This growth is partly by transfers, part new additions and attendance generally exceeds membership by up to 25%. There is clear market segmentation in church membership. The new churches represent a new market segment which after switching from other sub markets now means net Christian growth.

Why, then, could such a young organisation prove to be so effective, when such a large, well-established institution as the Methodist Church was declining so rapidly? There must be many factors at work here, but the flexibility of the new fledgeling churches was certainly one of the most significant. They did not have to contend with a preservation society!

Similar factors have been identified in the United States, where the Methodist Church declined by 18 per cent between 1965 and 1989. John Vughn of Southwest Baptist University compiled a list of America's fastest growing congregations and discovered that 445 of the 500 were outside the mainline denominations. Population and demographic shifts, he discovered, meant that long-established churches found themselves struggling along in unpromising locations.

In their book *American Mainline Religion*, Wade Clark Roof of the University of Massachusetts at Amherst and William McKinney of Hartford Seminary pinned much of the blame for decline on long-term demographic trends and the mainline churches' inability to respond to them.

Like the pioneering Methodists of the early eighteenth century, the new churches in Britain today are able to open up and function with little or no interference from a headquarters. Churches are started by those moving into new areas who identify a need. They do not seek permission from hierarchies, or delay their mission pending the arrival of trained personnel. They don't have to construct special buildings because the church slowly develops in the homes of its members.

Why, then, did the house church grow so rapidly during this period? Dr David Harper pinpointed an important growth factor in his observations of the British new church movement which he labelled 'vision':

> Vision is the grand design, the end result, the final picture. Vision is relevant in a secular or spiritual context. Secular equivalents are often called mission statements. Vision has to be shared and caught so that it is owned. This way a group of people can be motivated to work towards a common goal. Without vision there may be much activity but little sense of direction, with a maintenance mentality to the organisation.

Preservation societies may be good at conserving the past, protecting a heritage and restoring relics, but they are not good at developing vision. The kingdom of God is a visionary movement which is part of a dynamic community bound to the living God.

Which way for the church, then? Like Wesley, we must take care not to leave behind us those things which are central to our faith, our experience and our gospel. But there are other things, many other things, which have no kingdom value but which the preservation society wants us to carry with us. These things are built on the traditions of men and not the will of God, and they often exclude others from the kingdom. They may have served a different age, but they have long passed their sell-by date and need to be disposed of.

The church is not a people stuck in the past, but a people on the move; a pilgrim people, journeying with God. We must learn how to become a dynamic community which is constantly seeking the way ahead and looking for the next step. We must rediscover what the Bible means by 'church'.

The pilgrim people

The New Testament idea of church had nothing to do with preserving buildings, traditions or religious institutions. The word which Paul and the other New Testament writers used for 'church' was *ekklesia*. It is a word that survives in our language today – ecclesiastical – but there was nothing stuffy or traditional about it when it was first coined!

Ekklesia goes back to two words in Hebrew: *edah*, which was used for any important meeting of the nation, and *qahal*, which meant 'to summon' or 'to call together'. It was an action word, implying movement and impending change for a community for ever travelling from the old to the new. It was a word strongly associated with the Exodus, Israel's miraculous escape from Egypt and God's providential care for them during their long years on the journey to the Promised Land. Just as he had called the people of Israel to a journey of faith, he calls us to move ever forward to a new adventure with him.

In Acts we read how Stephen refers to the Israelites on Mount Sinai as 'the church in the wilderness'. The scholar Cerfaux argues that this passage shows the origin of the

Christian usage of the word 'church'. The word *ekklesia*, therefore, showed that Christians were the people who had been 'called out' to become the new Israel. They belonged to something new, and Jesus was the new Moses who was gathering his community in preparation for the last days. The church was a pilgrim people who were journeying to the promised land of God's kingdom.

In Ephesians 2 Paul reminds the Gentile community of how much Christ has done for them. They had been called out of the old life of sin and shame, guilt and failure, separation from God and the hopelessness of the Law. They had been called to a new life, a new relationship with God, a new kingdom and a daily adventure of faith. They were part of a community which was travelling from the old to the new.

> ...at that time you were separate from Christ, excluded from citizenship in Israel and foreigners to the covenants of the promise, without hope and without God in the world. But now in Christ Jesus you who once were far away have been brought near through the blood of Christ (Eph 2:12–13).

The church of God is a gathering of people who are making a journey together. It is a physical journey of people who accompany each other along the way. It is a spiritual journey of people on the road from darkness to light. It is a timeless journey from here to eternity. This church constantly responds to the changing demands of the journey, and this travelling people are always on the look-out for God to show them the way ahead.

It is time to close down the preservation society and to discover the joy of being a people on the move. The longer we try to preserve the past for posterity, the further we will lag behind. We must stop wasting time on things which

have no value and avoid preserving traditions which are
best buried. We are the pilgrim people, travelling on into
the unknown; we are the *ekklesia,* and the real adventure
has only just begun!

> Therefore, since we are surrounded by such a great cloud of
> witnesses, let us throw off everything that hinders and the sin
> that so easily entangles, and let us run with perseverance the
> race marked out for us (Heb 12:1).

DISCUSSION: A VISION FOR CHANGE

Icebreaker

Have you ever been to a vintage car rally, steam train
'bluebell line' or antiques fair? What kind of people like to
preserve things? Why?

What good things need to be preserved in the life of the
church?

What shouldn't be preserved?

Why?

Bible base

Many of the great Bible characters in Hebrews 11:1–40 and
12:1–3 displayed great vision, courage and persistence.
They wanted to see things change. Divide up the passage
and in groups of three or four choose one character and
discuss their story together.

Which would your character have found easiest:
preserving the past or pushing on to the future?

Why?

Discussion questions

- Which is most important – biblical authority, Christian experience or church tradition?
- Why are all three important?
- Why do you think Wesley and Whitefield's preaching was so popular?
- Why did the established church find it such a threat?
- Could preaching become important again?
- What should we be preaching today?
- How did Wesley get in touch with the unreached people of the industrial towns?
- Who is your church in touch with?
- Who doesn't it reach? Why?
- What were the main differences between Wesley's leaders and the leaders of the Anglican churches?
- What makes a good leader?
- How can the church find good leaders?
- Why couldn't the established church react to the demographic changes of the industrial revolution?
- What demographic changes are there in Britain today? How can the church best respond?
- Are there any significant new communities developing in your area? What should your church do?
- Why is vision important for any organisation?
- How do we test vision?
- What kind of vision do you have for your local church?

(The questions may be tackled in any order. It is not necessary to answer them all!)

CHAPTER 2

A Vision for the World

A changing society

At the end of one of the long dark corridors of the institutional church there is a room labelled 'statistics'. Push open the door, and inside you'll find a clerk charged with the most depressing job in Christendom – measuring the decline of the church.

The figures entered on long official forms all end up here: numbers collated by faithful clergy in countless vestries up and down the land; numbers of church attenders, members, baptisms, confirmations and communicants; numbers which track the slow demise of institutional Christianity in the United Kingdom.

From time to time the clerk at the end of the corridor collates the figures and takes them to committees to be pored over by men in grey suits. They will bemoan the state of the institution, construct optimistic statements, and deliver excuses for the demise of the church in wordy press releases. And, all the time, their focus remains on what is happening in the church rather than what is happening in the world.

Jesus commissioned us to go into all the world, not to tarry in the courts of institutional religion. Our burden should be for a lost society, not a declining religious movement. Our soul must ache for a culture running outside the will of God, not a church order running out of steam. Our prayer should be directed towards lost souls, not lost statistics.

The fact of the matter is that institutional Christianity has become a huge bore to millions of people in our society. The really interesting indicators are not about what is happening in our church, but what is happening in the world that passes it by.

There is ample evidence that British society is changing, if only we could be bothered to study it. Over recent years, for instance, televised religion has caused millions of people to reach for the 'off' button. Between 1963 and 1970 the audiences for the televised morning service, the religious discussion programme *Meeting Point* and *Songs of Praise* fell by 60 per cent, 40 per cent and 30 per cent respectively. It is clear that what was once relevant has become irrelevant and that what was once important has become unimportant. But why?

When my wife was in hospital several years ago she waited patiently for *Songs of Praise* to appear on the TV screen in the ward. As soon as the opening credits came up, the other women in the ward asked for it to be turned off. One would have imagined that, during days of uncertainty, *Songs of Praise* would have had its place. Were the patients looking for a word of comfort, or the familiar memory of a favourite hymn? No. Religion seemed an intrusion into their suffering. But why?

Institutional religion is a turn-off. Independent television reported to its religious advisers that when the God-slot ended the audience almost doubled from 22.4 per cent to 40.3 per cent of capacity. It would seem that, in a world of confusion and sorrow, few are interested in the Christian message. But why?

Our ability to catch society's attention and to speak with relevance seems to have declined alarmingly in recent years. The 'People's Service' on radio attracted an audience of 11 per cent of the adult population in 1964, but it had more than halved within six short years. The decline continues unabated. Institutional religion is not on the agenda. Society has switched off. But why?

While we commiserate with each other about our declining churches, we are failing to notice what is happening in the society around us, and to ask the question 'why?'. It can be fun to discuss the numerical indicators of institutional church life, and to play the denominational numbers game, but this is not where the action is.

Church denominations may rise and fall and count their relative success in percentage points, but what really matters is the impact they make on the society that they are called to serve. Our commission is to make disciples, not adherents; to invite men and women to follow Jesus, not to join a denominational structure; to go into all the world, not to stay and worry about the church.

Our impact on the belief systems of our society is diminishing at an even greater rate than our ability to make new church members. In just twenty-five years there was a remarkable change in the popular perception of Jesus. The Gallup survey of 1957 found that 71 per cent of those who responded believed Jesus to be the Son of God, while 9 per cent looked on him as 'just a man'. By 1982, however, a detailed research project undertaken by Leeds University revealed that only 43 per cent saw him as the Son of God, while 30 per cent saw him as an 'ordinary human being'. People have been turning away from a popular faith in Jesus by the million. But why?

Even more alarming is the shifting pattern of belief

among young people. In the twelve years between 1974 and 1986 there was a massive sea change in the views of teenagers. Statistics published by the *British Journal of Religious Education* show that in 1974 a total of 41 per cent of secondary school pupils felt that God was very real to them, but twelve years later it had almost halved to 22 per cent.

During the same period teenagers who found it hard to believe in God rose from 36 per cent to 56 per cent. Little wonder, then, that the publishers of the statistics noted a 'consistent, widespread and large drift away from the churches among secondary school pupils'. Perhaps, even more, the figures indicated a 'consistent, widespread and large drift' away from God. But why?

The process of secularisation

While we have been playing church and worrying about the decline of the religious institution, something dramatic has been happening in British society. While we have been asking ourselves how to make our services more contemporary and how to make our buildings more user-friendly, we have not noticed the changing belief systems in the society all around us.

Our failure is not in making the church more efficient, but in understanding what is going on in a world that is looking elsewhere for meaning. The name of the game is secularisation. The renowned sociologist Peter L. Berger defined this process as 'what happens when sectors of society and culture are removed from the domination of religious institutions and symbols'.

Secularisation is a tide of social change which is driving the institutional church out of the mainstream of community life and deep into the margins of society. The sociologist Wilson summed it up when he noted that religious thinking, practice and institutions have 'lost their social significance'. He concluded that the institutional church in England is 'losing direct influence over the ideas and activities of men' (and women).

The grass-root effect of such a change is well illustrated in the work of the leading sociologists Hoggart and Halsey. Richard Hoggart's description of Hunslet in the 1920s and 30s in *The Uses of Literacy* observed the way of life of the British working class. He noted the religious context in which many of them lived their lives when they said, 'We're 'ere for a purpose,' or, 'There must be some purpose or we wouldn't be 'ere.' Hoggart concluded that their feeling of purpose presupposed their belief in God and demonstrated that they had a religious perspective on life.

A. H. Halsey noticed that this had all changed by the 1980s. His *Change in British Society* looked back to the 1920s and he observed, 'I am struck by the integration of ordinary families with the moral traditions of the old class and Christian society. That moral structure has ebbed away fast under the assault of the classless inequalities and the secular materialism of the post-war world.'

While the institutional church has been concentrating on restructuring its committees, deleting sexist language from its liturgies and composing worship songs with more of a beat, the tide of secularisation has flowed on. The church has been pushed aside by its failure to face up to secularisation. It has failed to understand its mission field. While we've been playing church the world has passed us by.

We live in a post-modern age. The scene has changed, and the church lives in a new context. Frederick Jameson, in *Postmodernism, or the Cultural Logic of Late Capitalism,* observed that 'the cultural structure of feeling somehow crystallised in the great shock of the crises of

1973, the oil crisis, the end of the international gold standard, the end of the wave of wars of national liberation, and the beginning of the end of traditional communism – revealing a new landscape'.

The church doesn't live in this new landscape and fails to recognise that the world has moved on. No matter how trendy the vicar, how up-tempo the worship, how comfortable the seats, how spectacular the sanctuary, how quadraphonic the sound system, how attractive the worship band or how colourful the notice board – they will not come back. While we have put our time into playing church, we should have put more effort into understanding the world.

Some sociologists tell us that a society affects the development of religious thinking within it. Sometimes the tide of social change runs favourable to the development of religious movements, and sometimes it runs contrary to them. Otto Madun noticed that 'the structure of each society limits and orientates the possibilities of action and religion within it'. The tide has been running against the church, and society has become less and less favourable to institutional Christianity.

Some sociologists believe that the reason for this significant social change is the process of urbanisation and the emergence of settled urban communities. Wallis and Bruce suggest that while a society is becoming urbanised and is unsettled and less structured, it is actually favourable to the emergence of new religious movements. The growth of the Methodist Church in Britain during the industrial revolution is quoted as a prime example of this phenomenon.

Later on, however, when an urban society becomes more stable and settled, and the traditional aspects of community life are undermined, these religious movements tend to diminish. This would explain why, for instance, the

Methodist Church was able to prosper in the social transformation of the industrial revolution, but declined when the new urban communities became more settled.

Undoubtedly, the church's inability to relate to urban society has had a devastating effect on its influence and importance. The sociologist R.H.Tawney noted that 'religion has been converted from the keystone which holds together the social edifice, into one of the departments within it, and the idea of a rule of right is replaced by economic expediency as the arbiter of policy and the criteria of conduct'.

Alan D. Gilbert, writing in *The Making of Post-Christian Britain*, observed that the Methodists were able to attract thousands of labourers into their churches in the early days of industrialisation, but the Victorian working classes were virtually impervious to their existence. He concluded that such churches retained their relative position in society only by relaxing membership standards to accommodate the lowering levels of commitment and by improving methods of autogenous growth based on the Sunday school.

We have been so preoccupied with our declining church membership, diminishing congregations and disintegrating church buildings that we have not concentrated on the real problem we face. We have not recognised our inability to relate to the felt needs of men and women in settled urban communities.

What, then, are the characteristics of such communities? The great pioneers of urban sociology Spengler and Simmel, in their investigations into the nature of contemporary city life, have noted a distinctive mind-set among urban men and women. They describe it as 'rational, intellectual, blasé, cynical, and, above all, very much alone'.

Urban people don't want to play institutional Christianity any more. The game is over. The stumps are pulled. No matter how we strive to make the match more entertaining, the rules easier to follow or the stadiums more user-friendly, the urban citizen will continue to walk on by. Our most pressing need is to understand the psyche of urban life, and all our wordy reports about church life and worship will never equip us for such a task.

What is it that makes urban humankind so difficult to reach? Why is the mission of the church in the United Kingdom so difficult in this environment? How can we begin to unpack the challenge which faces us?

A supermarket of ideas

The church's effectiveness within urban culture has diminished because of the arrival of many other 'sources of meaning' and 'explanations of existence' for our lives. Berger, in *The Social Reality of Religion*, pinpointed this plurality of meanings as the driving force behind secularisation. Undoubtedly the growth of popular under-standing about science, philosophy, comparative religion and psychotherapy has brought into the public arena many other protagonists of meaning and explanation. Non-Christian religion in the United Kingdom will rise from 538,321 adherents in 1970 to a projected 2,430,000 by the year 2000. The growth of phenomena such as New Age thinking, star signs, meditation and alternative medicine has offered a plethora of new religious perspectives. In North America more than 1,200 newspapers carry astrology columns. A Gallup survey among British teenagers in the mid-1980s revealed that over 50 per cent of them believed that astrology worked in some form.

Nicci Gerrard, writing in *The Observer*, noted our

contemporary addiction to fate: 'We "fall" in love. Then out again. It was "meant". It's not our fault. Madness "descends". Meetings are "meant". Things "turn out" for the best or "just happen". It's a "foregone conclusion". It was "in the stars". We grasp at coincidences.' This plurality of meaning is the driving force of secularism and it runs contrary to Christian mission. Once, the church cornered the market on meaning, but now Christianity is seen as just one among many options. Urban men and women pick and mix their religious beliefs from a bewildering display in the supermarket of life. The church has failed to understand this tide of new religious interpretations.

Little wonder, then, that Berger observed the widespread collapse of the plausibility of traditional 'definitions of reality'. Clive Calver summed this up when he noted that religious views of truth have been progressively discarded as the church has cast a contracting shadow upon society. He concluded that the church's claim to be relevant and to present standards of truth for the whole spectrum of life has become less and less credible.

I have stood in church vestries from Perth to Penzance and heard people apologise for the low attendance at worship. The excuses are diverse and often highly imaginative. Every kind of weather from sun to snow seems to adversely affect church attendance. Poor congregations, I have been told, are the result of the popularity of the car, the new Sunday TV drama, the standard of living, the absence of war and the hardness of the local people.

While our minds are constructing such lame excuses, we fail to face up to the real problem. The challenge which confronts us is how we understand the psyche of urban men and women. How can we persuade them of the truth of Christianity over and above the diversity of religious meanings from which they can choose? While we focus on membership statistics we avert our gaze from where the action should be: out there in the big wide world.

The most urgent task is not how we can make the church more attractive, or how we can persuade people to come in. The real challenge is how to start a meaningful dialogue with the world and demonstrate the power of God for all to see.

Contemporary opinion polls continue to support the fact that while the church plunges into decline, society's interest in spirituality continues unabated. The MORI poll in 1990 revealed that 76 per cent of the population believed in God, 69 per cent in sin, 68 per cent in a soul, 60 per cent in heaven, 48 per cent in life after death, 37 per cent in the devil and 31 per cent in hell. The European Values Group Survey of 1993 showed that more people in Britain believe in heaven than in life after death! This demonstrated that people 'elect to hold beliefs that allow them to have their cake and eat it too' (*New Statesman*, 1993).

The debate about explanation and meaning rolls ever onward in our society. The question is, how can we, as contemporary Christians, enter into it? More importantly, have we something meaningful to say? The Oprah Winfrey show screened in Britain as I write covered religious experience. The three guests talked of angels, out-of-body experiences and transformation by the light; but when members of the audience proposed a traditional Christian view of spirituality Oprah declared, 'I don't want any religion on this show.'

What do we have to say to a world which is fascinated by religious questions but disinterested in traditional answers? How can we challenge an existentialist world in which what is true for you is true, and what is true for me is true? How can we relate to an age in which I am expected to accept your truth as true as well as my own? As Clive Calver observed in *The Truth about Truth*:

> Today it has become common to assume the validity of many pathways to God, to deny the existence of absolute truth, and to extol the significance of multi-faith worship. This may sound a comfortable theory, but it bears little resemblance to reality. It reduces truth to the level of individual belief determined by personal experience. Any notion of absolute truth is rejected – it would simply not exist.

We have lingered in the safety of our religious ghetto for too long. We have spent too much time preserving our safe haven of church life. The way forward is the way out into secular society. We must make our pitch for truth in the supermarket of religious perspectives. We must move out of maintaining an institution and move into effective mission. We are not commissioned to stay in the temple courts of church life, but to go out into all the world and proclaim that Jesus Christ is the truth.

Is it possible that the institutional church is not the best instrument for such a task? Are we expending too much effort in trying to make something relevant which is long past its sell-by date? Perhaps we are fiddling while Rome burns, rearranging the deck-chairs on the Titanic, and resetting the bones in the graveyard. It is time to move on, for the institutional church has had its day.

In a well-respected study of popular attitudes to religion as far back as 1947, Victor Gollancz noted that the institutional church was getting out of touch with the people. He concluded:

> Both in regard to formal observances and general attitude, the younger generation shows a much more critical outlook... Criticism and disillusion centre chiefly on organised religion,

on the churches and their dignitaries, on the ostentatious practice of religion, rather than on religion itself.

Which way for the church, then? A membership drive? A good public relations firm? An ecumenical superchurch? A slim and efficient religious machine? No. We must rediscover that the church is the people of God, and the people of God belong out there in the real world.

The temple in the world

Whether we like it or not the church in Britain is seen as a religious institution. We project an unfriendly image through our austere, crumbling buildings. We live as though God dwells in bricks and mortar. Such structures inhibit our mission, shape our thinking, drain our resources and occupy our time.

Is it possible that the more time and effort we have expended on institutional Christianity, the more we have shut people out? Have we been so preoccupied with the work of sustaining religious institutions that we've stopped working on the real building – the people of God?

In the Old Testament the people of God were a nomadic tribe on their way to the Promised Land. They recognised that God lived among them in a special tent which was known as the tent of the Lord's presence. The Bible teaches that following the death and resurrection of Jesus, however, God lives in the lives of ordinary men and women. Those of us who are committed Christians are, quite literally, the house of God.

Paul reminded the Corinthians of this when he taught that Jesus is the foundation, church leaders are the builders, but the people of God are the temple. God does not live in a tent, a chapel, a cathedral or a religious institution. He lives in his people. We carry his presence into the world wherever we go. 'You realize,' Paul wrote, 'that you are the temple of God, and God himself is present in you? No one will get by with vandalizing God's temple, you can be sure of that. God's temple is sacred – and you, remember, *are* the temple' (1 Cor 3:9, *The Message*).

I write this in a seventeenth-century villa in the mountains of Provence in southern France. The house is a tall, rambling structure built into the mountainside and literally miles from anywhere. As I drove up the rough mountain track towards the house, I saw a large gap in the front wall which revealed a massive stone rock: a cornerstone. The whole building was constructed around it. I don't know why the builders chose to leave the stone exposed, but it's a lovely reminder that the whole house is built around something completely immovable and secure.

The church is built on an unshakeable Cornerstone who is Jesus Christ. All who are committed to him are the stones of the building. Together we form the temple of God: 'Welcome to the living Stone, the source of life. The workmen took one look and threw it out; God set it in the place of honor. Present yourselves as building stones for the construction of a sanctuary vibrant with life, in which you'll serve as holy priests offering Christ-approved lives up to God' (1 Pet 2:5, *The Message*).

It is a tragedy that many of us have spent so much time building a religious institution when the New Testament teaches that God lives in his people. Billions of pounds would have been better spent in shaping the lives of the living temple than in holding together the bricks and mortar of a fading religious institution.

Paul told the Ephesians that they should not feel like strangers in the holy place, for they themselves were

God's building, the temple.

> God is building a home. He's using us all – irrespective of
> how we got here – in what He is building. He used the
> apostles and prophets for the foundation. Now He's using you,
> fitting you in brick by brick, stone by stone, with Christ Jesus
> as the cornerstone that holds all the parts together. We see it
> taking shape day after day – a holy Temple built by God, all of
> us built into it, a Temple in which God is quite at home (Eph
> 2:19–22, *The Message*).

Which way for the church of the new millennium? A
church built with people who live in the real world, with
every member a powerful witness to the living God. John
Havlik was right when he said that the church is never a
place but always a people; never a fold but always a flock;
never a sacred building but always a believing assembly.
The church is we who pray, not where we pray.

Our failure to reach secular Britain is due to a failure of
our theology. We have been building a religious institution
and have become completely preoccupied with it. We've
lost our nerve and ceased to be a living temple standing tall
for all to see. The challenge is to become a church joined
mysteriously with all other Christians. We must become the
living temple, and recognise that each brick and stone is
valuable, integral and beautiful. The key to mission in a
secular society is not more emphasis on the religious
institution, but more involvement in the real world. There
can be no threshold barrier here, because there is no
threshold. Wherever Christians are, they are the temple.
Wherever believers pray, they are the house of prayer.
Wherever they worship, they demonstrate the glory of God.
They are the church in the world. This is the way ahead –
not more buildings, but *the* building.

We must change our focus and lose our preoccupation with a denominational institution. We must stop hiding from the world behind the high walls of our dark sanctuaries. We must become a living, being, active body in the midst of society. We must stop looking at the needs of the institution and start looking to the needs of the people we are called to serve. The church must function in every work-place, street, hospital, school-yard and neighbourhood in the land.

If we really do become the living temple, people will no longer have to decipher illegible script from fading noticeboards to find out who we are or what we're called. They will see us functioning in the mainstream of life. Christians will have come out of hiding and will be the living temple.

So the way forward is to leave behind our religious culture, our crumbling edifices and our institutional way of doing things. These things are nothing more than cumbersome baggage and will not help us in our mission. Let us discover what it means to be the living temple in the world.

DISCUSSION: A VISION FOR THE WORLD

Icebreaker

Hand out pages from TV listings to the group.
  Which programmes would you turn off immediately?
  Why?
  Why do so many people switch off televised religion?

Bible base

Read Ephesians 2:19–22.

What did Paul mean by a living temple?

Where does God live?

How is it built?

Who is part of it?

What is a church?

Discussion questions

- Have you noticed any changes in society towards institutional Christianity? What were they?
- Is institutional religion a turn-off? If so, why?
- Why do you think that the views of young people changed so dramatically over such a short time?
- 'Our commission is to invite men and women to follow Jesus, not to join a denominational structure.' Do you agree or disagree?
- Is there a clash between the agenda of the church and the agenda of the kingdom of God? If so, what is it?
- Have you ever wanted to take someone to church but were afraid to do so? Why?
- What aspects of secularisation have you noticed during your lifetime?
- Has the church failed to understand what is happening in the world? If so, what evidence is there for this?
- Is urban community 'rational, intellectual, blasé, cynical, and very much alone'? If so, why?
- What message does the church have for such a world?
- Give examples of the religious beliefs which people whom you know pursue. Do people pick and mix their religious beliefs? Why?

● Is it possible that the institutional church isn't the best instrument for mission in a secular society? If so, what should replace it?

(Feel free to range over the questions in any order. It's not crucial to answer them all!)

CHAPTER 3

A Vision for Mission

Paralysis

Total paralysis is one of the most torturous conditions in human experience. The paralysed person knows what he wants to do, but his body doesn't respond. He reaches out to take hold of something, but his arm doesn't move. He knows where he wants to go, but his legs won't take him there. He wants to be self-sufficient, but he is dependent on others for the most mundane tasks. Life is a patchwork of small frustrations.

Derek Sheane of ICI, in his *Symptomology of Bureaucratic Breakdown,* describes a kind of paralysis which is often present in the business world. It is called 'co-ordination paralysis', and it permanently disables many companies and institutions. The outcome is that such organisations find it a struggle to move at all. My twenty years as an ordained minister have led me to conclude that the institutional church is suffering from a bad case of co-ordination paralysis. In my experience, the ecclesiastical machine is high on paperwork but low on action.

Sheane suggests that business paralysis occurs when a company smothers initiative and discourages decision-making. The hallmark of a paralysed organisation is that nothing new can happen without the permission of its many interconnected parts. Anyone who has struggled to launch new initiatives in the church will recognise such a syndrome. The institutional church thrives on 'checking things out with its interconnected parts'. Any department in a paralysed business has the power to stop initiatives which emerge from another section by using its power of veto to slow things down. In the paralysed denominations, a bewildering hierarchy of committees, boards, councils and commissions exerts a continuing resistance on new experiments in mission. It is undoubtedly a negative influence on the life of the church.

Consensus

Carlo Ricci, in a detailed examination called 'The Hidden Games of Organisations', suggests that the different groups involved in making decisions in an organisation may have very different 'levels of reality'. He concludes that 'at least three interconnected factors lead to interactional slow-down in a system. The number of parts, components or players; the nature of the interdependence among them; and the amount of uncertainty affecting their behaviour.'

It follows, therefore, that it will take an organisation longer to make a decision if there are a lot of people involved in discussing new ideas and especially if they hold divergent views. Little wonder, then, that in an institutional church dominated by committees it sometimes seems easier to make no decisions at all.

In the Anglican communion, power often resides with the local vicar. If he or she does not have a commitment to mission or a vision for action, the church can be held back. The Baptist and Free Evangelical model of a local eldership also has its drawbacks, for several elders can hold widely differing views. The tension among them can be uncreative and it can smother vision. In the Methodist Church a proposal must wend its way from the local church council to the circuit meeting, through the district committee to the synod and then up to the church's annual conference. Along the way countless other power-brokers have the chance to amend, defer, rationalise or reject the proposal. New ideas rarely survive the process, for they are smashed to pieces on the jagged rocks of church bureaucracy.

The problem is accentuated when those involved in the church's decision-making process each have their own priorities. The national umbrella organisation is likely to distance itself from anything which might be divisive and will usually sacrifice innovation for the sake of unity. In his classic book *Group Processes,* Martin F. Kaplan concluded: 'Groups for whom cohesion is important for attainment of other goals will be interested in maintaining harmony, and thus will be sensitive to deviations from consensus or norms.' The denominational churches generally move forward by consensus. They discourage revolutionary action because they fear it strains internal relationships. Instead, they keep everyone busy maintaining the status quo, and there is always plenty of institutional housekeeping to do. This activity is focused on improving the organisation itself rather than on developing its effectiveness in the market-place.

The church of the new millennium must learn to deplore such management by consensus. It must find the space to release young leaders to try new things, and to give them encouragement to innovate. It must help visionary entrepreneurs to discover that their time has come, and that their new ideas are welcomed with enthusiasm and a willingness to take risks.

The great missionary exploits of church history have never been managed by consensus. They have usually been developed by lone pioneers who have seen a vision and preferred to die rather than deny it. There are such people emerging within the young leadership of the church, and the church must begin to identify them, encourage them and value their contribution. These visionaries hold the key to the church's future development, and by nature they are impatient people. They will not wait while large organisations store their vision in filing cabinets, or while committees wait endlessly for a consensus. If they do, the moment will have passed and the opportunity will have been missed.

The church of the new millennium will not move forward by consensus but by a recognition of rich diversity. When it learns how to release visionaries to come up with new ideas it will begin to discover that it really does have a future!

Bureaucracy

Charles Handy, in his book *Gods of Management. The Changing Work of Organisations,* suggested that 'traditional' institutions are too preoccupied with tidying up their own procedures to respond to the changing world around them. He observed that organisations with a long history of continued success with one activity live as though things will always continue as before. They assume that the more they rationalise, codify and standardise, the more effective they will be.

When John Wesley chaired the early meetings of the Methodist conference, the agenda was small and the rule book thin. Today, the agenda runs to hundreds of pages, and the list of rules looks like a phone directory. This organisation, like denominations such as the Salvation

Army and the Anglican Church, seems to need constantly to rationalise, codify and standardise.

In many denominations the body of Christ has been paralysed, and the people of God have been immobilised. Traditional church institutions bear all the hallmarks of organisational paralysis. The church is the living body of Christ, but denominational organisations put it in a strait-jacket. It is administered by boards, committees and middle-managers whose agenda is focused on the life of the institution. As a result, the church just doesn't have the time to set out its stall in the secular market-place of religious ideas.

The denominations have failed to respond to the changing scene around them. They have disregarded the divine commission to 'go into all the world'. No properly managed business, charity or service industry would have been allowed to continue for so long in such an irresponsible way.

Dr David Harper is a lecturer at the University of Hallam Business School, and a local church leader. He noted that church attendance in England declined at the rate of approximately 1,000 people per week between 1979 and 1989 and observed that Methodist membership declined by a staggering 11 per cent over the same period. In an extensive study of the problem he concluded:

> If a profit-making organisation lost customers at the rate the church has lost members then there would be a thorough review of products and organisation, heads would roll and new strategies be implemented. Clearly customers have lost faith in the product and the church, and question its relevance and credibility. The church, like any other organisation, should face its own responsibility for this decline and not blame external circumstances.

Sadly, the traditional church denominations haven't undertaken a searching review of 'products and organisation'. No new strategy has evolved; no goals have been set; no targets identified; no plans implemented. The haemorrhaging of church life has continued unabated while the traditional denominations have been paralysed to respond.

The denominations have been too busy restructuring their committees, rewriting their rule books and reordering their budgets to respond to the secularisation of the society around them. They are dominated by the 'nothing new' syndrome which Sheane summed up in the phrase: 'Bureaucracies polish but do not invent. This applies to both processes and products.' The churches have been too busy polishing to have time to invent. Nothing illustrates this more clearly than the church's response to the New Town movement of the 1960s and 70s. Here was an unparalleled opportunity for innovative mission and for planting contemporary church models without the encumbrance of a long local tradition. Sadly, the denominations were too encumbered with their institutional machinery to respond effectively.

The demographic and social change stirred up by the New Town movement should have been favourable to the work of mission. It certainly created fertile ground for John Wesley's mission in the eighteenth century. The Revd Sinclair Walker, writing in 1967, noted that there had not been such a tremendous reshaping of the nation's life since the industrial revolution. He urged that the church be mobilised to meet the needs of the vast New Town communities.

Certainly the demographic changes created by the New Town movement were significant. Between 1946, when the first New Town was designated, and 1976, when the

Commission for New Towns was wound up, a total of twenty-nine New Towns were designated. By 1976, with many of the towns still well below their targeted populations, almost one million people had settled in them. This happened during a period of continuous numerical growth in the United Kingdom, for between 1951 and 1970 the population increased by over 5 million. With such a major increase in population, one might have assumed that church membership would have grown substantially. Population growth and demographic movement, factors which were favourable to the development of early Methodism, were both present during this period, but the decline in Methodist membership continued unabated. Between 1951 and 1970 600,000 people were housed in New Towns, and the Methodist Church declined from 741,596 members to 601,068. Its ability to make new members sank from just under 30,000 to just over 11,000 per annum.

Although most church leaders would argue that the kingdom of God cannot be measured in statistical terms, it is clear from the archive material available that the churches which were developed in New Towns did not do well, and that many of the problems stemmed from the institution's reticence to allow experimentation.

In a well-argued paper to the Annual Conference of the New Town Ministers Association in 1974, Mr Ian Gray, the Managing Director of Skelmersdale Development Corporation, observed that the churches were unable to react quickly enough to the needs of the new communities because their established procedures inhibited swift decision-making. He concluded: 'Perhaps we in the Development Corporations are too impatient, but I know our impatience is shared by many individual clergymen and churchgoers.'

From 21st to 24th April 1971 the New Town Ministers Association held an unusual conference entitled 'Shechem'. It took the form of a three-day game based on an imaginary New Town called Shechem. The participants were asked to study extensive papers relating to the pretend-town ahead of the conference and to join various planning groups during the event. The game highlighted the tensions between the planning authorities, the local church ministers and denominational institutions.

One of the independent observers present at the conference was Brian Goodey of the Centre for Urban and Regional Studies at the University of Birmingham. He said:

> I've been very distressed, I think as one must be if one has read through all the reports, to see the emphasis on 'hardware', on the massive millstone which the church has around its neck – both in terms of buildings and after this morning's session in terms of structures. I got completely lost, not being 'in the club', as to where all these organisations really fitted in. There seemed to be an awful lot of committees upon which one could actually serve but very little actually happening.

Two years later, in 1973, the New Town Ministers Association annual report noted that there were still intense feelings of frustration with the institutionalised church and that these had surfaced at their annual conference. There was a strong feeling that the church in the New Town situation was continuing to struggle under handicaps which were largely of its own making. The report noted that 'when planning surveys have been carried out and detailed proposals made, too often they have been shelved due to the lack of a sufficiently authoritative body to carry them out'.

If the denominations had moved into the New Towns and founded churches of different styles and cultures all over the area, their mission would have been more effective and less time-consuming. If they had expended their energies on planting congregations matching the people groups of the area, the whole process would have been far more effective. New Towns should have provided an arena for experiment and innovation in the life of the church. Unfortunately, many of the original concepts put forward by church planning groups were smothered at birth by leading officials and boards. In Milton Keynes, for example, there was clear support from the different denominations for a very experimental and innovative form of church life. Sadly, however, the Methodists withdrew from this movement under the influence of the Methodist Circuit, District and Head Office, and the initiative had to be scrapped.

In *Managing in Enterprise Contexts,* Bill Richardson of the Hallam University Business School labels certain decisional processes 'garbage can models'. He describes processes which have people acting before they think and which create outcomes that emerge in the absence of leadership direction. He describes this process as 'organisational outcomes emerging from an interplay of problems, solutions, participants and choices'.

Time and again in my study of New Town mission I have been forced to the conclusion that things were organised from the 'garbage can' model of management. There was little evidence of any clear strategy. Bureaucratic styles of church government seem to inhibit change and progress rather than enhance it. The church of the new millennium must allow people on the frontline to get on with mission rather than tying them up in ecclesiastical knots.

Strategy

G. A. Cole, in *Strategic Management,* suggests that forecasting is an essential ingredient in any effective enterprise. He defines it as any attempt, usually based on past performance, to predict future outcomes and trends in the environments of an organisation. It is a process which is crucial to limiting the risks involved in devising and implementing a strategy.

Charles Handy, the management analyst, suggests that some organisations stagnate because they do not form a future strategy. He believes that this short-sightedness stems from the predictability of their role. Churches fit his definition well, and their long-established 'role culture' tends to make them backward-looking and inert. He writes:

> It is a misconception to believe that managing means decision-making in the 'role culture'. Decisions are in fact few in number and are very much in the processing category. It is the design of the organization's railway system which is crucial: its operation only requires an adherence to timetables. Administration is a word that fits 'role cultures'.

Many churches, both nationally and locally, have focused on an adherence to timetables, not on questions about what kind of trains should run or where they should go. These 'role culture' institutions are reticent to develop detailed strategies for the future, or to measure their effectiveness in real terms.

In 1994, a Bible Society survey revealed that 60 per cent of the different kinds of church in its sample lacked any sort of 'vision statement'. Presumably they were too busy polishing to have time to develop new strategies for growth. Few churches look at what is happening in society around them or try to predict what will be. Fewer still seem able to develop any kind of response to a changing world or to develop a strategy for future mission. The church isn't good at forecasting.

The American business historian Alfred D. Chandler defined strategy as the determination of the basic long-term goals of an enterprise and the adoption of courses of action to achieve them. If big business considers strategy important for making money, the people of God should see it as vital for their primary work of mission.

An extensive survey of the ecumenical process in the New Town of Skelmersdale revealed that there was hardly any strategic planning. The plans for a new church seemed to emerge in a completely re-active rather than pro-active way. The Revd D. H. R. Jones, secretary of the New Town Ministers Association, in reviewing the early days in the Skelmersdale church plant observed: 'A reasonably managed business would ask a good many detailed questions before agreeing to put £60,000 into something. The Church of God, no doubt with commendable faith, does not seem to think this necessary!'

The Revd Jones went on to undertake a comprehensive survey of the decision-making processes used by the churches working in New Towns in January 1970. He was anxious to discover whether the churches were making decisions about their mission from the earliest stages of the development of the New Town master plan. He discovered that only a pitiful 12 per cent of New Town ministers had an overall mission policy and concluded that policy in New Town churches was conspicuous by its absence. The church, locally and nationally, was too late and too indecisive in making its plans for work in the New Towns. The New Town Ministers 1970 report, 'Planning for Mission', called for fresh action and outlined a basic formula which all churches operating in New Towns

needed to follow. It urged each church to decide what kind
of mission it proposed to undertake, and encouraged them
to set defined goals to express their mission in greater
detail. It was clear to them that mission was the church's
greatest priority in the New Towns and that each church
needed a strategy in order to be effective. My research,
however, led me to conclude that this appeal was unheeded
in many of the New Town contexts. The church's mission
lacked a strategy.

Mission

The church does not like change, and would prefer to use
well-worn models than to try anything new. Institutional
paralysis is often evident in the life and work of the
contemporary church.

Every local church should regularly examine its strategy
for mission to its neighbourhood, identify new possibilities,
and create plans promoting growth. Each minister should
fight the kind of institutional paralysis which prefers to do
the same this year as last. Every local church and national
denomination should be evolving a developing strategy for
its ongoing mission. If the church doesn't plan for success,
it might as well plan for failure!

Emil Brunner once said that the church exists by mission
in the same way that a fire exists by burning. Lesslie
Newbigin went further by suggesting that a church which
has lost its missionary vision is not an authentic New
Testament church. The churches of the United Kingdom
must stop anticipating decline and start planning for
growth; they must move from maintenance to mission.

John Skoglund, in *To the Whole Creation*, argued that
mission can never be thought of as just one of the
characteristics of the church. It is *the* hallmark

of the church, for mission is at the heart of what the church is. The Great Commission isn't one church activity among many, but the church's most essential activity.

A hospital is a lot of things: it is a hotel where people are housed in comfort; it is a restaurant where hundreds of meals are served daily; it is a communications centre where the switchboard handles dozens of calls an hour; it is a business office where records, accounts, flow charts and job descriptions are kept; it is a training centre where doctors, nurses and other medical personnel increase their skills. But above all else the hospital is a place where people are healed. This is its essential activity.

The essential activity of the Christian church is leading men and women to Christ, and all its other functions are secondary. Mission is the core activity of the church's business, but often the churches don't have a strategy for doing it. The denominational church is paralysed and the body of Christ is locked in a strait-jacket.

A Bible Society research project in 1994 attempted to discover if local churches were committed to evangelism. The commission of Jesus commands us to go and 'make disciples', and one might have assumed that evangelism would have topped the agenda of every local church. This is not so.

A representative sample of 400 Protestant ministers and church leaders in England and Wales was selected, and 203 responses were received, representing 51 per cent of the total. Out of the total replies, a staggering 65 per cent admitted that local evangelism was not high on their agenda, and 67 per cent did not see that the primary purpose of the local church was to share the good news of Jesus with their community.

Even more depressing, over half of the sample admitted that they did not have a regular programme of local evangelism, and over half said that their congregation would be uncomfortable with such a programme. Almost 70 per cent revealed that there was no regular training in evangelism available for their people.

The compilers of the survey used the responses to estimate the relationship between mission and maintenance in local churches. They were forced to conclude that only one-third of the group was mission-orientated.

In a review of church business meetings the survey revealed that churches spent an average of less than 15 per cent of their working time on local evangelism. Well over a quarter of the churches spent less than 5 per cent of their committee time on mission. Most revealing of all, 49 per cent of the sample spent 5 per cent or less of their budget on telling others about Jesus.

The traditional denominations in the United Kingdom are paralysed. This is seen in slow-moving ecclesiastical structures and the church's lack of response to a changing culture. It is illustrated by the ineffectiveness of the church in New Towns, by a lack of vision for mission and a paucity of resources for evangelism. The cumbersome ecclesiastical giants are asleep, and it's time they were woken up!

The body of Christ

You may be able to survive without an arm or a leg, a finger or an appendix, but you would not survive long without a head. The head co-ordinates, controls, facilitates and empowers the various parts of the body to fulfil their different functions.

The body of Christ works well when it lives under the authority of the Head, and the paralysis of the church is caused by its lack of submission to the Head. The members of the body are not receiving the right signals, not running in co-ordination with each other, and not submitted to the will of him to whom the body belongs: 'He is before all things, and in him all things hold together. And he is the head of the body, the church; he is the beginning and the first-born from among the dead, so that in everything he might have the supremacy' (Col 1:17–18). Every part of the body of Christ, be it a struggling local congregation or a national church institution, must be submitted to the Head and living under the lordship of Jesus Christ. Every part must respond to his will and fulfil his agenda, for this is the way out of paralysis and the way into action.

Which way for the church, then? We must shake off the strait-jacket and discover what it means to be free. We need to move from paralysis to mobility; from inertia to action. We must become a co-ordinated team all playing on the same side. There is no argument between two legs as to which one should step out first, or between four fingers as to which one will point the way. Paul wrote, 'The body is a unit, though it is made up of many parts; and though all its parts are many, they form one body' (1 Cor 12:12).

The symptoms of paralysis are not only evident in the corporate life of the church, but also in the lives of individual Christians. The people of God in Britain today are paralysed people wherever they don't respond to God's call for mission and witness. The body of Christ has been locked in a strait-jacket. Some parts of the body have been paralysed by structures which have sought to control, restrict and manage them. His people must be released to take part in the work of mission. We must drop the hierarchical models of church life which paralyse individual action and local initiative. The local church is at the cutting edge and must be free to respond to the changing scene. The denominational role is to empower and release the local people for mission, not to keep them in line.

Kevin Giles, writing in *What on Earth Is the Church?*, pinpointed the kind of tension which exists between local churches and their governing institutions:

> ...ecclesiastical bureaucrats in denominational headquarters and some theologians are prone to claim that somehow the corporate denominational church is prior to, or more important than, the local congregation ... congregations can exist and thrive without being part of a larger community of Christians grouped into a denominational framework, but a denomination cannot exist without congregational life.

The church won't move forward by consensus, by committee or by systems of government which are looking for the safe majority. It will advance by initiative, by risk and by obedience to the one Great Commission. Christ rules the body, not some man-made organisation. He knows the way ahead, not us. Every aspect of the church's life must be submitted to his authority: 'And God placed all things under his feet and appointed him to be head over everything for the church, which is his body, the fulness of him who fills everything in every way' (Eph 1:22–23).

Paralysis comes when parts of the body fail to function. A damaged spinal cord can lead to paralysed legs. A broken arm can restrict the movement of the hand. Blind eyes or deaf ears slow down the body's effectiveness. Those parts in the life of the church which aren't functioning need major surgery if the life of the body of Christ is to be a life of co-ordinated response towards common goals. Each member must play their part and fulfil their responsibility. Each believer must be appointed and equipped to fulfil the particular role in the body which is theirs, and theirs alone: 'Just as each of us has one body with many members, and these members do not all have the same function, so in Christ we who are many form one body, and each member belongs to all the others. We have different gifts, according to the grace given us' (Rom 12:4–6).

There is nothing institutional about the working of this body because it's joined together by deep bonds of compassion and care. Paul's parable makes the point. When the tooth aches, the whole body suffers. When the finger has been cut, the body's defences are marshalled for healing. When the heart aches, the eyes shed tears. The people of Christ share a deep sense of interconnectedness which the world can never understand.

The body of Christ doesn't work properly without this rich sense of belonging. If this was missing it would live without feeling, without sensitivity and without caring – a body paralysed. 'If one part suffers, every part suffers with it; if one part is honoured, every part rejoices with it' (1 Cor 12:26). If we really are the body of Christ we must discover the rich sense of belonging that he created us for. No part of the body has any greater worth than another. 'On the contrary,' Paul writes, 'those parts of the body that seem to be weaker are indispensable....'

There is a dearth of biblical understanding about the body of Christ in the denominational churches. We appoint people to jobs instead of discovering their God-given role in the body. We push them to do things that are not part of their calling or for which they are not equipped. We misuse the resources which God has given to his church. We call people to serve the processes of a dead institution rather than the commission of a living God.

There is much for the people of God to do, for together we represent the life of Jesus here on earth. He has a massive agenda to complete, and we are the people through whom he wants to work. We must take the institutional strait-jacket off, and be free of this organisational paralysis. We must become the body of Christ.

Which way for the church, then? To be the body of Christ: all connected; all functioning; all healthy; all co-ordinated; all released; all working together.

DISCUSSION: A VISION FOR MISSION

Icebreaker

Do some simple co-ordinated aerobic exercises, followed by others which demand a lot of bodily co-ordination.

Talk about co-ordination. Do some in the group find bodily co-ordination difficult? What problems does this create?

Bible base

Read together 1 Corinthians 12:12–27.

Ask: How should the body of Christ operate in practice? How do we submit to the Head? What is your ministry within the body?

Questions

● Name some great missionaries or evangelists from church history. What was their relationship to the church institution?
● Did they have a wide consensus of support?

- How did the institutions treat them?
- How are innovative and high-risk ideas received in your local church?
- Are you aware of any new ideas in your church or denomination which have failed to draw a consensus?
- What happened to them?
- How can we encourage visionaries and entrepreneurs in mission?
- 'Bureaucracies are too busy polishing to have time to invent.' Does your local church do this?
- Does your denomination have a clear strategy for growth?
- If you were to create a three-point strategy for your denomination (or stream), what would it be?
- What would you most like to see the local church doing in its mission?
- What three aims and goals would you identify as the most important strategy for your local church?
- How can we help to release the church from its straitjacket?

(Feel free to range over the questions in any order. It's not crucial to answer them all!)

CHAPTER 4

A Vision for Growth

The sower

If you want a good harvest, don't let a statistician sow the seed. He will stand in the autumn furrow and try to calculate the chances of the seed surviving. He will anticipate chill winds, heavy snow and frozen earth, and he will forecast a poor harvest, if any harvest at all.

If you want a good harvest, don't use a pollster to sow the seed. He will stand, opinion poll in one hand and calculator in the other, and compute the chances of a crop. He will canvass public opinion and decide that harvests aren't popular any more. He will examine the food-markets of the world and conclude that there is insufficient demand, so he will recommend that harvest be cancelled.

If you want a good harvest, don't ask a committee to sow the seed. They will stand at the edge of the field muttering disapprovingly to each other and protecting their pristine green wellingtons from the mud. Committees cannot sow without a majority, and as they rarely agree on anything majorities are hard to find. They will conclude that the soil is poor and the prospects bleak, and they will vote that the seed not be sown, at least not this year. Besides, they are in a rush to catch the next train back to London.

If you want a good harvest, don't employ an agricultural expert to sow the seed. His diploma in soil management, his degree in farm technology and his doctorate in agrarian history have not prepared him for such a task. He sits at his computer and produces complex graphs projecting the failure of the crop, but he never sows seed himself. He never ventures out into the field or feels the rich dark soil running between his fingers. His thesis argues that harvests are a thing of the past and that seed-sowing is no longer worth the effort.

But somewhere beyond the grey boundaries of the urban sprawl a sower goes out to sow. He barely understands the process, let alone the depressing predictions of the experts. He throws the raw seed into the prevailing wind and his heart is full of hope. He is driven by a conviction too deep for words and he knows that, against all odds, harvest will surely come.

Within the mainline church denominations seed-sowing has been out of favour for more than a century. It is little wonder that there is no sign of harvest.

The Methodist Church switched its energies from pioneer evangelism among the new urban working class to the Christian education of its members' children. Most of the traditional mainline denominations have demonstrated a similar weakness. They have cared too little about reaching those outside and failed to develop strategies of evangelism which might have led to new growth. The denominations have cultivated market gardens, not cast raw seed onto barren land.

Decline

Decline among the traditional denominations is nothing new. The Free Church membership figures in England during the late 1930s demonstrate a decline of about 1 per cent per year, and this rate of decline roughly trebled from 1937 to 1947, the period of the Second World War. The position stabilised in 1950, but the decline continued at the end of the 1950s and accelerated during the 1960s and 1970s.

These figures don't really portray the true extent of the decline, however. During this period there was a significant change in the relationship between church membership and church attendance. Before 1914 it could generally be assumed that the numbers attending Free Church worship were two or three times as great as those formally in membership. In later years, however, attendance was generally less than the recorded membership.

These figures must also be set in the context of continued growth within the English population as a whole, so the influence of the Free churches was declining even more rapidly than the membership figures indicate. In the early 1980s the leading Free churchman Rupert Davies noted the psychological effect of this massive decline:

> In the 1930s people began to feel that the problems of the 1920s were not merely transient, but had deeper causes; yet there remained an underlying optimism. In the 1940s, despite and partly because of the war, there were hopes for renewal and revival which were not entirely disappointed in the early 1950s. But by the later 1950s people began to feel that things would not improve, and in the 1960s and 1970s decline came to be accepted as normal; even to maintain membership figures was regarded as an achievement. There was therefore a slow but immense change in non-conformist psychology.

Church membership measures an important sociological phenomenon. In *The Elementary Forms of the Religious*

Life the eminent sociologist Emile Durkheim observed the religious community and concluded: 'The individuals which compose it feel themselves united to each other by the simple fact that they think in the same way in regard to the sacred and its relations with the profane world, and by the fact that they translate these common ideas into common practices, in what is called a church.'

Durkheimian sociological theory emphasises, therefore, that religion is the expression of a community and so 'rites are means by which the social group reaffirms itself'. When membership declines, then, the movement or organisation affected begins to weaken. Individuals who become church members are publicly stating their affirmation of a particular group, but those who terminate their membership are effectively helping to dissolve it. The decline in church membership demonstrates, according to Durkheim, that fewer and fewer people in Britain 'translate their common ideas into common practices in what is called a church'.

The seed has not been sown, and the harvest has not been reaped. Fewer and fewer people have been willing to commit themselves to church membership because they have not heard the gospel, understood it, accepted it, or come to believe it. The decline of the mainline denominations has resulted from their appalling lack of vision, pioneer evangelism and effective strategy. The churches have failed to persuade those outside to adopt their 'common ideas and common practices'.

During the 1970s the Methodist Church lost a total of 20 per cent of its membership, 13 per cent of its ministers and 14 per cent of its church buildings. Church attendance in the nation as a whole continued to decline and the publishers of the National Opinion Poll in 1982 stated: 'Relative to the total population very few people in Britain attend church or are active members: about one adult in five goes once a month or more and about half do not go at all except for weddings and funerals.'

Some would argue that the concept of church membership is out of date, but until some other way of registering commitment is discovered it is the only way of measuring church growth or decline. Certainly, the national media viewed the 1996 Methodist membership statistics as an important indicator of decline. Banner headlines in several national dailies declared messages such as 'Methodist Meltdown'. For several days it was impossible to open a newspaper without seeing lead articles predicting the extinction of this long-established church. The Leader in *The Independent* on 22nd March observed, 'Push the curve of membership forward into the next century and the mainstream Christian church – the denominations with hierarchies and centralised structures – effectively comes to an end. In contrast, the decentralised, theologically promiscuous fringe churches, often lumped together as "fundamentalist", show signs of vitality.'

The Guardian reported the Revd Brian Beck, Secretary of the Methodist Conference, as saying, 'There is no point running away from it, we must face the decline and its very important consequences. If it goes on at this rate, we will not be able to maintain the structure of the church.'

The Independent quoted the Revd Peter Barber, Methodist Church Membership Secretary: 'There is an institutional time bomb ticking away. The annual rate of decline is gradually accelerating. The picture is similar whether we examine rural, small town, suburban, inner-city or city-centre churches.' He went on to foresee a 'dismantling of the central structures of the denomination'.

Andrew Brown, reviewing Methodism's annual 2.5 per cent decline in *The Independent*, suggested that the church lacked a coherent strategy:

The United Reformed Church, itself formed from a merger of smaller congregationalist bodies, is shrinking almost as fast as the Methodists, and hopes for salvation by union with them. The Methodists, in turn, seem to have no real long-term strategy beyond union with the Church of England – but that body, too, is facing similar problems and for similar reasons.

Columnist Mary Kenny, comparing the death of the traditional Christian denominations with the rise of Islam, declared: 'What does British Islam offer in its [Methodism's] place? Perhaps not much on the music front so far, but characteristics which seem to be draining out of some aspects of Christianity. Commitment. Conviction. Energy. Values. Belief. Certainty.'

If you want a good harvest, do you send out a sower without a strategy or employ a farmer who lacks commitment, conviction, energy, values, belief or certainty? Perhaps the statisticians, the pollsters, the committees and the experts have been left in charge of the farm for too long. The church has lost sight of harvest.

An authentic gospel

Some researchers trace the decline of Methodism to the demise of the class meeting and the breakdown of authority over its membership. They sense that the flame of spiritual revival which produced such amazing growth in the early years flickered out. Robert Currie, in his uncomfortable review of Methodist history and ecumenism, described some of the changes in spirituality and church practice which occurred at the end of the nineteenth century:

Gradually they extricated themselves from traditional doctrines and creeds. They began to construct a much looser, vaguer and more palatable Christianity... Religion was a permanent Sunday School Anniversary, Christ the affable minister, the universe a tidy church hall full of happy faces. Traditional Christianity was dead.

The trend of decline is equally apparent in the United States, as mainline denominations lose millions of members to the evangelical groups. It is interesting to note what social observers say about these trends.

Richard Ostling wrote in *Time* magazine in May 1989:

Explanations abound. No doubt cultural and demographic changes have eroded mainline churches. Constant organization reshuffles have taken a toll. In addition far too many mainline churches are lacking in the marketing and communications savvy that the Evangelicals employ to win new members... A preoccupation with political and social issues at the expense of good old-fashioned faith has alienated many members. Not only are the traditional denominations failing to get their message across; they are increasingly unsure what that message is.

Another American, John Naisbitt, writing in *Trend Reports* which monitors social trends in 6,000 US periodicals each month, also noted the decline of mainline denominations and the growth of evangelical churches, and concluded:

As a society, we have been moving from the old to the new. And we are still in motion. Caught between eras we experience turbulence. A very important point is that the strictest and most demanding denominations, especially the Southern Baptists, are growing fastest – while the liberal churches continue to lose members. This should not be surprising. During turbulent times many people need structure – not ambiguity in their lives. They need something to hang onto, not something to debate. The demand for structure will

increase – supplied not by the old established denominations –
but by the great array of new native grown fundamentalist
faiths.

The only established church to record encouraging patterns
of growth in recent years is the Baptist Church. Baptists
grew by 2 per cent from 1985 to 1989 after a decline in the
previous six-year period. In their detailed assessment of
Baptist Church growth in England, under the title *Turning
the Tide,* Paul Beasley-Murray and Alan Wilkinson echoed
these American observers:

> Growing churches seem to be those, predominantly, that are
> expecting great things from God and have that conviction
> underlying all their activity. Church Growth is not simply
> doing the right things at the right time. It is also a matter of
> being a fellowship which believes that it is God's plan for his
> church to grow and having the conviction that he wants it to
> happen in that particular church: it becomes a matter of faith.

Dr Os Guiness, the controversial lecturer at the
Williamsburg Charter Foundation in Virginia, warned the
Lausanne Congress in Manila, 'We have tried to use the
forces of modernization to serve us, but unwittingly we
ourselves have been shaped by them. We have set up
endless patrols to detect the dangers of the world in our
societies, but the devil has trundled this new worldliness
right past our eyes and into the church.'

It would seem that the people of our secular society are
not interested in a bland, gutless, undemanding religion,
and they are not looking for confusion. If these observers
are to be believed, the church's attempt to make
Christianity more acceptable has made it unpalatable. If we
are to challenge the false assumptions of a materialist age
we must present the authentic Christian message without

compromise. If the gospel is to meet the needs of individuals in our society we need to tell the whole story.

A harvest vision

The harvest vision recognises that the gospel is like a tiny mustard seed with a growth potential which far exceeds our understanding. It understands that the gospel is like a seed growing silently, whose development is certain but whose growth cannot be measured. The gospel is a seed which, when planted in good soil, bears a harvest thirty, sixty or a hundredfold. Harvest theology teaches that 'the harvest is plentiful but the workers are few' (Mt 9:37).

Jesus stood in the wintry field when there was nothing to see but bare earth and barren land and declared: 'Do you not say, "Four months more and then the harvest"? I tell you, open your eyes and look at the fields! They are ripe for harvest' (Jn 4:35). He was looking at the empty field with the eye of faith and could see that it was ready for reaping. He could see the crop not yet grown, the bountiful harvest yet to be. He looked beyond the collapse of time and saw the distant future when the sower and the reaper would rejoice together.

The mission field may look bare and barren, but when the seed of the gospel is scattered, it releases the potential for harvest. The one who sows is not called to be successful, only faithful; not called to look back at what might have been, only to look forward to what will surely be; not called to make gloomy predictions about the outcome, only to sow in hope. The sower must never feel despondent, for in the providence of God there will surely be a harvest.

Sowing has been out of fashion for too long, and those who should have scattered the seed preferred to stay at home. We need a new vision of harvest to be birthed in us by the Holy Spirit. It won't come through changes in denominational policy but when we wait on God and seek his will. It flows from an outpouring of his love.

Although the harvest vision is given by God, the principles of church growth are concepts which must be studied and understood. Church growth was first developed in the USA in the early 1960s and initially the discipline was taught to those training to go overseas as missionaries. Those involved soon realised, however, that the practice could also be used within mainstream American churches.

Later, the British Church Growth Association was formed, which defined its work as investigating the nature, function, structure, health and multiplication of Christian churches. It aimed to combine a study of the principles of growth in the Bible with related insights from the contemporary social and behavioural sciences.

Donald McGavran, in *Understanding Church Growth,* defended the group's preoccupation with numbers. He argued that the church is made up of countable people and that there is nothing particularly spiritual about not counting them! He pointed out that the numerical approach is used in all kinds of human endeavour, including industry, commerce, finance, research, government and invention, and concluded that much of human enterprise is developed by continual measurement.

Church growth experts believe that regular surveys of churches should be undertaken to check their spiritual health. McGavran compared it to a nurse using a thermometer to assess the patient's temperature: the thermometer will not help the patient to get better, but it is a tool which can help the diagnosis. In the same way church growth surveys don't help the church grow, but they give an assessment of a church's health so that an intelligent diagnosis can be made. The world's leading church growth experts all suggest that once such a survey has been completed, the local church can begin to set its goals for future action. It can begin to develop its strategy for growth.

G. G. Hunter writes: 'A local church may enjoy growth for a while without sophisticated organising and planning if something contagious is spontaneously occurring in its ministry or outreach. But effective year-by-year outreach and growth will only take place through a congregation organised for programmatic outreach.'

Strategists advocate a variety of methods for developing growth in the life of a church. There is *internal growth*, in which Christians within a church become better disciples. This is often a quality growth rather than a numerical one, but it may mean that some people within the life of the church find Jesus as Lord and become committed Christians. We must never forget to evangelise within the church as well as outside of it!

Then there is *expansion growth*, when a church decides to get out among the unchurched in its community and to win them for Christ. These new disciples are nurtured in the context of the local church. Many church-based missions and guest services work on this principle and continue to be effective. Every church should be doing this kind of outreach as part of its normal ongoing programme.

Extension growth occurs when a church identifies a specific group of people who have no Christian witness among them. It aims to become incarnate within the group, to share Jesus with them, and to plant a church among them. This is a demanding exercise, for it will usually mean that a group of church members will have to go to live and work among this community. This kind of mission, however, is generally considered to be the most effective evangelistic method of all. Many of Britain's most successful house churches have used this model extensively.

Finally, but most difficult of all, *bridging growth* occurs when a church seeks to start new churches in a culture different from its own. It means that the pioneer church-planters involved will have to become more deeply involved in their new culture and leave behind many of their former ways. They may have to learn a new language, develop different social aspirations, and get alongside the local people. It could take a lifetime.

These church growth concepts are anathema to many in the traditional denominations. They would rather predict decline than plan for growth. Let the statisticians, the pollsters, the committees and the experts say that the church cannot grow; let them cast the dark shadow of doom over the future of church life; let them declare that there is no hope. They lack a theology of harvest.

The rest of us must seek God for growth. We must seek personal and corporate renewal as the inspiration for such a movement. We must study what makes churches grow and understand what strategies are most effective. We must get sowing!

The homogenous unit

One of the most controversial yet most effective styles of church uses what is called 'the homogenous unit principle'. It was a concept first propounded by McGavran, who declared that people like to become Christians without crossing racial, linguistic or class barriers.

Robinson, another church growth exponent, suggested that churches which express a single culture or social group can often penetrate a people group most effectively. The gospel, and the church that flows from it, are effectively enculturalised.

But what is culture? One recognised definition states that it is an integrated system of beliefs (about God, or reality, or ultimate meanings), of values (about what is true, good, beautiful and normative), of customs (how to behave, relate to others, talk, pray, dress or work) – and of institutions which express them. This is what binds society together and gives it a sense of identity, dignity, security and continuity.

The homogenous unit principle is about incarnating the Christian message in terms of nationality, ethnicity, age, sex, race, culture, language and social class. It is about starting churches within cultures rather than dragging outsiders across denominational thresholds and into an alien land.

In order to become a Baptist, a Methodist, an Anglican or whatever, the incomer generally has to learn the right language, wear the right clothes and express themselves in the right way to be accepted by the rest of the group. According to the homogenous unit principle, the new church starts where the outsider is at, not where the denominational church would like him to be.

Clive Calver of the Evangelical Alliance pinpointed the alienating effect of church culture on some of those whom we are trying to reach: 'This is a class-ridden nation, and the Christian faith has become a middle-class religion. It is seen in practice as irrelevant to the working man. We need to free our faith from its cultural entrapment.'

For generations, the church has constructed its mission strategy geographically. It has drawn parish boundaries, stationed ministers in defined communities, and done its mission in the streets and neighbourhoods around its traditional buildings.

Alan D. Gilbert, in *The Making of Post-Christian Britain*, sees the rise of this urban culture as one of the major challenges to the church in the secular society.

> Organised religion, everywhere in the British Isles, has failed to cope with the decline of the territorial community and the emergence of pluralistic, partial communities. The idea of territoriality remains central to Christian planning, both pastoral and evangelistic, and church leaders still tend to think of work among newer, functional communities as 'special ministries'... they remain peripheral in relation to overall effort and expenditure in all the major denominations.

Communities are changing, therefore, and people don't think of themselves as belonging geographically to a specific area. They belong to people groups and relate to others with whom they share a lot in common. We must start to see communities as clusters of people groups, not as rows of streets or lines of houses. A people group is a significantly large grouping of individuals who perceive themselves to have a common affinity for one another. This bond may develop because of shared language, religion, ethnicity, place of residence, occupation, class or situation (such as common adversity). It is a real bond, however, and it ties people closely to one another. The people group is the contemporary way of being a community.

Nearly all of our cities operate in this pluralistic way. Different groups within a defined area maintain their own traditions rather than adopting a standard form of behaviour. Each group has distinctive gifts to offer and a form of equality develops which is based on sharing rather than on adherence to a dominant ethos.

Dr David Hillborn, the minister of City Temple in London, believes that our post-modern society will continue to develop in this way. He argues that the small group or the 'micro-community' is the archetype of post-modernity. Modernism put its faith in mass education, whereas post-modernism stresses that people can learn most in small cells and sub-cultures. The people group is the future way of living, and the cell church is crucial for the church of the new millennium.

Jordan Bishop didn't mince words when he wrote: 'If conversion to Christ implies cultural or religious alienation, our gospel is distorted, and we are, perhaps paradoxically, preaching a human gospel, imposing our own ethno-centrism on the people to whom we preach.' It should never be necessary for new Christians to have to leave their culture to join a church. We need to reach people with a gospel which enables them to develop a pattern of Christian community and lifestyle which matches their people group. We must not ask young people to wear suits, expect *Sun* readers to enjoy sermons, invite yuppies to sit in cold sanctuaries, or demand that Radio One fans sing hymns.

The apostle Paul declared, 'To the weak I became weak, to win the weak. I have become all things to all men so that by all possible means I might save some' (1 Cor 9:22). The gospel is universal in its message, but in its application it has to be moulded to the homogenous group of the receiver. The church of the new millennium must be moulded too. And the churches of the future must take on the multiplicity of shapes of the people groups within our society.

The cell church

The common feature of growing churches is their extensive use of the small homogenous group. It is nothing new, for this was the hallmark of Wesley's early Methodism, and it was called the class meeting.

John Walsh concluded that Methodism was able to weave together into a connected system all kinds of little 'marginal outcrops and expatriates'. It was a movement of small people groups within the new towns of the industrial revolution, and it grew quickly and haphazardly. It was this simple process which enabled Methodism to grow by a staggering 4.5 per cent in 1770 alone! There was a lack of co-ordinated action in the early days of the denomination, but this was a primary reason for its rapid growth. It was easy for members of different people groups to join the movement and to feel that they belonged. The class meetings held Wesley's followers together and formed the backbone of the movement. Wesley quickly saw the potential of such groups. 'This is the very thing,' he declared, 'the very thing we have wanted so long.'

The first class meetings gathered by accident rather than design. The financial needs of the rapidly expanding organisation, with its plans for new buildings and commitment to the poor, called for some method of collecting funds. Many of the members were too poor to afford a penny a week, but the leader of each class called weekly on each member of the group, looked at their living conditions, collected the pennies of those who could afford to pay and often made good the deficit himself.

At first the class leader visited the members of his class individually in their homes, but when this proved difficult the class gathered together. When they gathered, the groups began to discuss the social, ethical and religious problems of their daily life. Gradually the class meeting became a regular feature of Methodist life. A book on the subject, published in 1889, concluded:

In the early days of the movement thousands of converts in various parts of the United Kingdom needed religious instruction and care. No adequate provision, scarcely any provision at all of ordinary pastoral oversight was possible. Class meetings did much to supply that great want, and thereby gave cohesion and permanence to the work.

Under the direction of Wesley and his assistants the men and women who led the classes watched over their people. They were aware that at any time they might be called to give an account of their pastoral oversight.

Wesley recognised the effect of the classes on his followers. He wrote:

It can scarcely be conceived what advantages have been reaped from this little prudential regulation. Many now happily experienced that Christian fellowship, of which they had not so much an idea before. They began to bear one another's burdens, and naturally to care for each other. As they had daily a more intimate acquaintance with, so they had a more endeared affection for each other. Evil men were detected and reproved: they were borne with for a season; if they forsook their sins, we received them gladly; if they obstinately persisted therein, it was openly declared that they were not of us.

The class meeting allowed a group of people who shared the same culture to form a Christian community which related to their common needs and expectations. Sadly, the organisational culture prevalent in many churches today alienates the very communities which they are seeking to serve.

Schein (1985) talks of organisational culture as 'a pattern of basic assumptions invented, discovered or developed by a given group as it learns to cope with its problems of external adaptation and internal integration that has worked well enough to be considered valid, and to be taught to new members as the correct way to perceive, think, and feel in relation to those problems'. Sadly, a church's organisational culture can make it completely unapproachable to those who pass its doors. Those involved in frontline mission have often felt desperately frustrated when they have tried to incorporate people into a congregation which alienated outsiders by its organisational culture.

The report of the Evangelical Alliance New Towns Study Group called 'Evangelical strategy in the New Towns', published in 1971, identified the same problem:

> There is a cultural gap between the typical evangelical Christian and most of the people in the New Towns... It is substantially a gap created by us to protect ourselves from a living encounter with unbelief... We are sure that if we continue to duplicate the suburban churches where we have so far managed to hold on to fairly healthy numbers, it will not be a work that God is demanding of us. It will have been a retreat into what we already feel secure in, rather than an adventure with God in what He is wanting us to do in New Towns.

The sociologist Anthony concluded:

> Cultures develop in communities which are distinctive from their neighbours and are held together by patterns of economic and social cooperation reinforced by custom, language, tradition, history and networks of moral interdependence and reciprocity. As these are established and sedimented over time they lead to customary understandings and obligations, patterns of expectations that do not require to be calculated or defended.

The churches of the new millennium need to grow up within and become part of such cultures if they are to be relevant and welcoming.

One of the best ways of influencing a people group is to form a cell of about twelve people within it. The group should consist of several committed Christians who are culturally attuned, and several members of the people group who are open to hearing more about Jesus. Gradually this group forms a fellowship cell and becomes a witness within the wider community of the people group.

Wang Ming-Dao, a Christian leader in China, teaches that where there are Christians, there is a church. He believes that, even though there may only be a few people present, they are a church.

According to Jim Montgomery of the Dawn 2000 church-planting movement, any small group of Christians led by an elder and meeting on a regular basis for worship, instruction, sacraments and service can be called a church. The Vineyard Church calls these cells 'kinship groups'; the house church Ichthus names them 'neighbourhood groups; Pioneer churches label them 'home church'. Perhaps the most well-known prototype is the Alpha course established by Holy Trinity, Brompton.

Whether the leaders recognise it or not, this kind of cell group is basically a mini-church, and Christian conversion happens within the group as a process, with non-Christians joining the group and gradually accepting the message of Jesus. They in turn invite their non-believing friends to join another group, and in this way the church self-perpetuates, forming a new cell group with each cycle.

Such small groups allow for the contextualisation of the church because each group can be focused around different sorts of people. Young people, single parents, the over-sixties, people from a specific ethnic background, prisoners and ex-offenders, divorced or singles, executives, scientists, students, artists or those with a more working-class or upper-class background are just a few of the many possibilities.

I believe that the church of the new millennium will be a church of many small groups. Some of these groups may meet on church premises, and be drawn from different ethnic or socioeconomic backgrounds. Some may meet in a tightly zoned geographic area, where two or three couples who get on well begin to meet together and to form their own neighbourhood cell. Other groups may share a specific interest, background, workplace or experience. The cells will demonstrate their different cultural preferences. At present, for example, many church leaders are unashamedly middle class, and their theological training has segregated them from the working-class culture of which they were once a part. As a result genuine expressions of working-class culture are rarely found in mainstream church life. Jeffrey Harris, writing in the 1977 Methodist Home Mission Report, stated:

> ...all the evidence available to us makes plain that there is a deep estrangement between institutional religion and the urban working class, and especially the semi-skilled and unskilled. Here is a missionary task which Methodism has scarcely identified and yet needs urgent attention. We need to learn from the Church overseas and see that this requires an expression of faith in working class cultures, and there is scarcely any section of our institutional life which will not be affected.

Those who feel alienated from middle-class Christianity will find that, at last, their contribution will be valued and affirmed. There will be room for those who prefer gut reactions to concepts, and worship that is more from the heart than from the mind. There will be space for those who prefer rhythm to plainsong, and for those who relate to feelings more than words.

The new church will recognise and affirm the many ethnic communities in the country. About 9 per cent of the population are first- or second-generation British residents. Yet many Christians within the ethnic community don't find today's average English church either helpful or relevant. Research indicates that it is only middle-class black people who make a home for themselves in denominational churches. The new millennium church will affirm ethnic groups as they develop their own worship styles, use their own language and draw on traditions from their own cultures. The church will recognise that Christianity doesn't have to wear Western clothes. Ethnic cells will function autonomously, but be closely connected to the Christian village.

The new church will recognise that young people can no longer wait for leadership or be patronised by their elders. They will be empowered to create their own styles of worship and communication, and be released into the gifts which God has given them. Young people will find space to pray in their own language, sing their own rhythm, affirm their own leaders and celebrate their own faith. The Young People's Working Group at the Nationwide Initiative in Evangelism regretted that 'the churches have not provided an atmosphere or a place which can receive the respect of young people and does not cause them to lose face with their peers'. This place will be provided at last. Cells of young people will develop their own initiatives for mission, explore their own styles of worship and work out their own response to the needs of the world. They will not be allocated occasional youth services because they will be developing their own relevant worship week by week.

From the diversity of the different groups which meet separately for worship will come a richness and strength. St Paul summed it up when he wrote, 'Where the Spirit of the Lord is, there is freedom' (2 Cor 3:17). Styles of worship are only vehicles for adoration and praise, and some will be carried into the presence of the living God by noise and movement, others by silence and stillness. There will be room for everyone in the Christian village, and none will have the right to judge which is the best.

The growth of all-age worship is one of the most significant trends in the last twenty-five years. Churches which were once deeply committed to the Sunday school now structure their worship life around the children. This will continue, but they will also understand that kids need space to develop their own worship in their own particular way. Different age groups have their own preferences and expectations. We can't expect children to grow in Christ if they are not given the kind of context which will enable them to develop where they're at and to enjoy worship experiences suited to their own age and culture. Children will often worship apart from their parents in their own liberated and noisy way.

Peter Selby's challenging book *Belonging* opposes tribalism in the church and exhorts us to a new openness:

We have been offered a world where participation is by achievement and competitive entry, and for over a decade seen our society irresistibly drawn to it. The Church's own life… has become a gigantic process of collusion with those who believe such a world to be desired. We have joined in an exercise in holding on, in excluding those who might endanger our way of seeing things, and the privileges we have come to enjoy. In such a Church, in the midst of such a world, it is easy to stop seeing the essential attractiveness of those people and gifts we reject. There is nothing about them to be longed for; for they are only a threat and a danger.

The church of the new millennium will be a church of many welcomes, where diverse people groups will find a place of their own in the rich family of God's people. We will, at last, see the essential attractiveness of those we have rejected and we will begin to value them.

The new church, I believe, will become a federation of local cell groups. The entrepreneurial leader may act as an apostle over the cells, but the cells will operate fairly autonomously. They will meet together regularly for worship, and could form a network of leaders to provide a cover of accountability for the local movement. The emphasis will be on releasing individuals to start new cells rather than on holding them in to those which are already established. There will be a great deal of pain as the denominational churches try to free themselves from the traditional models of church life and become part of what God is doing among his people.

In John we read how the shepherd and the sheep belong to one another, united in a bond of mutual knowledge and trust (Jn 10:14, 27). The communal nature of discipleship is stressed in John 17 where Jesus prays for his followers that they may be 'one': one with each other, and one with the disciples of all time. Luke's understanding of the early church was that it was very much a new united community. He speaks of them being 'united' (Acts 2:46; 4:24; 5:12; 8:6; 15:25) in a spiritual oneness. This oneness of heart is most clearly seen in the practice of holding 'all things in common' (Acts 2:44; 4:32) so that there was not a needy person among them (Acts 4:34).

The church of the new millennium will be a church of many small communities of people who will belong to one another. They will evolve their own worship styles, means of outreach, Christian education and mission. From time to time the different cell groups will join together for the breaking of bread and for large-scale celebratory worship.

Roger Greenway, in *Discipling the City,* argued that the church's evangelistic task demands that every apartment building have a church faithful to God's word established in it. And Donald McGavran summed it all up when he wrote: 'The goal of the Great Commission... is the establishment of a cell of committed Christians in every community, every neighbourhood, every class and condition of people, where everyone can hear and see demonstrated the gospel from his own intimates, in his tongue, and has a reasonable opportunity to become a disciple of Jesus Christ.'

This, then, is the challenge of the harvest: to go to where the people are, to sow the seed, and to see the harvest grow within their culture, their people group and their community – not to drag them into our long-established denominational churches and out of their comfort zone.

Donald English, in his visionary booklet *Into the 21st Century,* pointed out:

> One of the great strengths of church planting is that it enables us to find new venues, to welcome new people, to have the opportunity to discover new ways of being the people of God, in our worship, our fellowship, our service and our witness. Churches need to regard these new congregations not as daughter churches who will one day grow up but as 'sister churches' from the very day they come into existence.

The church must plant cells if it is to grow in the new millennium. It is time we stopped playing our denominational games and stopped protecting our traditional church cultures. It is time we threw the seed over the barren, untilled field and let it grow in the soil where it lands.

The multi-celled church of the new millennium may not be one which we recognise, but God will recognise it, for it will become a community of his people. It will grow quickly, as each cell transforms the people group of which it is a part. If we sow in this way, there will surely be a mighty harvest.

DISCUSSION: A VISION FOR GROWTH

Icebreaker

Get some different kinds of seed and sow them in small pots as a group. Talk about seed, harvest and growth. If there are some gardeners within the group, get them talking about some of their proudest and most disastrous moments.

Bible base

Read Matthew 13:1–43.

What spiritual principles do these parables teach about seed, soil, sowing and harvest?

If you had to compose a press release about the future of the church based on these parables, what would it say?

Discussion questions

● How do you feel when you read that the church is in decline?

- Are these feelings from God or from ourselves?
- Is church membership an outdated form of registering commitment? If so, what should replace it?
- What do you feel about Mary Kenny's statement that commitment, conviction, energy, values, belief and certainty are characteristics which are draining out of Christianity?
- Would you feel sad if the 'central structures of the denomination were dismantled'? If so, why?
- What might replace them?
- Discuss the four different kinds of church growth: Internal, Expansion, Extension and Bridging.
- Give examples of what your church might do to grow.
- Are we being unrealistic in expecting people from other cultures to enter church life?
- Why do you think the homogenous unit principle is so divisive?
- Why does it work so well?
- How would you feel about belonging to a church of homogenous cells?
- Do you believe that the cell church could prove a way of enabling the church to grow?
- How could you begin to develop a cell strategy in your locality?

(Feel free to range over the questions in any order. It is not crucial to answer them all!)

CHAPTER 5

A Vision for Leadership

The one man band

There is a musician whose skill is legendary, but whose music is appalling. Few others can match his ability, but the end result is excruciating. He is the one man band, and he is the star act of carnival parades and street theatre presentations all over the world. He carries a bass drum on his back and cymbals between his knees. There is a mouth-organ suspended in front of him and a trombone in his hand. From time to time, in perfect rhythm, he beats the big bass drum with a drumstick strapped to his elbow. He is a spectacle to watch, but agonising to listen to!

His counterpart is found in the life of many contemporary churches, and he may be called vicar, minister, priest, elder, deacon or leader. Whatever his title, the role is much the same. He is the one man band, trying to do six things at once and doing none of them particularly well. His ministry is a discordant cacophony, and he expends much energy to little lasting effect.

The church has come to rely on one man bands such as this to do much of its work. It places layers of responsibility on shoulders not built to carry them. The leader struggles from day to day trying to do the work of administrator, evangelist, pastor, caretaker, worship leader, diplomat, civil servant, preacher and prophet. Meanwhile, the congregation watches, for they are spectators, not participants.

This was not the early church model of Christian leadership. There is no biblical evidence to support the idea that the work of the church is to be done by paid professionals who are 'good at everything'.

No, the role of the leader in the New Testament was not to do the work himself, but to envision, equip and empower others to join him in doing it. The early church taught that all the members are the *laos* – the people – who have been called out of society to serve God and others. There was to be no hierarchy or different levels of status because all the believers were part of the church's mission and belonged to the people of God. Peter made it clear that everyone is a member of the team when he wrote: 'But you are a chosen people, a royal priesthood, a holy nation, a people belonging to God, that you may declare the praises of him who called you out of darkness into his wonderful light. Once you were not a people, but now you are the people of God' (1 Pet 2:9–10).

George Newlands, in *The Church of God,* noted that 'the purpose of the whole Christian community is "diaconia", service, and in this sense there is a priesthood of all believers. This service is entirely dependent on Christ, and on his continuing ministry through the Holy Spirit.'

The writer of the Acts of the Apostles made it clear that the early church was a community, and that everyone needed to make their contribution towards it. All the church members seemed to experience a strong sense of community and responsibility towards one another: 'Every day they continued to meet together in the temple courts. They broke bread in their homes and ate together with glad and sincere hearts' (Acts 2:46).

The emerging church does not need more multi-skilled people to do much of its work on their own. There is no room for the one man band school of leadership in the church of the new millennium. We must change the expectations of local churches which still look for such a person. The key to a healthy and growing church is not a superstar leader but a team of local Christians who are all empowered to play their part in the church's life.

Kevin Giles concludes in *What on Earth Is the Church?*:

> Nothing seen in the New Testament has endorsed the view that the ordering of the church was given from the start, or that the threefold order of bishops, priests and deacons was known in the first century. This means that the church is not defined by its ministerial structures; it is defined by its communal existence given by God in Christ, and by the presence of the Spirit who provides the leaders needed.

The early church was not a parade of one man bands. The letters of leaders like Peter and Paul were full of encouragement and inspiration to local people to fulfil their own ministry and to develop their own priestly role: 'You also, like living stones, are being built into a spiritual house to be a holy priesthood, offering spiritual sacrifices acceptable to God through Jesus Christ' (1 Pet 2:5). The biblical concept of church leadership is not based on the 'star performer', but rather on the leader who enables and facilitates each of the people of God to fulfil their calling. Leadership is not about status in the hierarchy, but about servanthood to the body. 'There are different kinds of gifts, but the same Spirit,' wrote Paul. 'There are different kinds of service, but the same Lord. There are different kinds of working, but the same God works all of them in all men.

Now to each one the manifestation of the Spirit is given for the common good' (1 Cor 12:4–7).

Wesley's leaders

John Wesley's ability to plant hundreds of new churches in the burgeoning new towns of the industrial revolution lay not in his personal ability to see through the process, nor in the recruitment of an able team of clergy. He was able to develop a nationwide network of 8,000 class leaders who shared his vision. These leaders were the movers and shakers of his generation. They were not one man bands, but envisioners and enablers.

This loosely connected network of volunteers was the team Wesley chose to raise up hundreds of new congregations in the new towns of the industrial revolution. These leaders were drawn from the people groups of the new industrial communities and experienced all the fears, struggles and aspirations of their contemporaries. They were not isolated from the community, but a product of the culture in which they were working.

The leadership style exercised by Wesley nationally may have been autocratic, but when it came to local mission he gave the local people real freedom to pioneer new work. Wesley trusted his leaders to develop their own strategy for mission. They were not working to some ideology gleaned from a theological college far away, but working out their strategy in among the people of the industrial towns.

Sociologists have been fascinated by the way in which Wesley was able to raise working-class people to exalted positions of leadership in his societies. His class leaders exercised a personal and energetic pastoral care among the Methodist members. They were in regular contact with their people, and cared for them with a deep sense of concern.

There was no glamour about being a leader in early Methodism, for it was often a dangerous and soul-destroying job, and it lacked social status. Wesley's itinerant preachers moved from village to village with a vision to set up more and more autonomous but connected congregations.

These leaders exercised a refreshingly different style of leadership from that which many working-class people had come to expect from the established church. In many communities the parson was dependent on the squire – a dependence which was often an economic as well as a social alliance. As a result, the parson generally cared for the rich and powerful more conscientiously than he cared for the weak and oppressed.

The bishops also modelled a kind of detached, one man band style of leadership. They generally did what they wanted in the dioceses, many of them spending two-thirds of the year in London, not daring to miss voting time at the House of Lords. Commitment to the London scene was vital if they wished to rise to the higher echelons of church life. Their ministry was not about empowering others but rather about claiming power for themselves.

Whatever their rank, therefore, the Anglican clergy seemed most concerned with the preservation of their own position in the power structure, their own domination of church life and their own status in society. They had little time or energy left to envision the people of God or to help them survive in the social turmoil of the industrial revolution. The eighteenth-century Anglican clergyman was a prime example of the one man band school of ministry.

The established church could not raise a leadership team to match the commitment and enthusiasm of Wesley's volunteer preachers. Their ordained leaders were too concerned with tradition, security and safety to risk their lives for the kingdom of God. They were too hungry for the fading glory of human acclaim to suffer for the eternal glory of the kingdom of God.

The early Methodists were so committed to Wesley's vision for lay participation that they had it enshrined in the very legal framework of the Methodist Constitution. The Deed of Union Clause 4 states:

> The Methodist Church holds the doctrine of the priesthood of all believers and consequently believes that no priesthood exists which belongs to a particular order or class... but in the exercise of its corporate life and worship special qualifications for the discharge of special duties are required and thus the principle of representative selection is recognised.

Motivators

The denominational churches often see the development of their mission as being the duty of paid professionals. They rely too heavily on the one man band, which is a resource in scarce supply. Little effort is put into motivating the laity, who are the key to local church growth. The pressure on the denominations is to find sufficient professionals to maintain existing work, and this means that they can rarely release personnel to start anything new. There just aren't enough one man bands to go round. Whatever leaders are available are used for the maintenance of the church's existing work rather than for the development of new opportunities. The church just doesn't have enough paid personnel to develop new work at the cutting edge in unchurched areas.

Robin Gill noted that

> The Church of England continues to deploy a quite

disproportionate number of its clergy in rural parishes. Today the village population is only a fifth the size of its Victorian population and ninety per cent of the British population as a whole is urban, not rural. Yet the Church of England still deploys half its stipendiary clergy in rural and small town situations.

Such an institution finds it difficult to send clergy to pioneer work in highly secularised and deprived urban areas because its work-force is not trained for such a task. Their hermeneutics, New Testament Greek, pastoralia and liturgical skills have only prepared them to be a one man band in a traditional parish church, where they will be warmly appreciated by an elderly cluster of religious traditionalists.

Sadly, the concept of the 'priesthood of all believers' so tenaciously defended by the traditional denominations is rarely seen in practice. The report of the Ministerial Training Policy Working Group of the Methodist Church in 1996 was forced to admit as much.

Since ordained ministers or presbyters are focusing all the common life and responsibilities of the whole church there is a danger not only that they will be seen to be the church more than those who are not ordained are perceived to be, but that each of them will have to enact every part of that life and those responsibilities. Allied to a growing sense of individualism in our culture, this has tended to produce the ideal of the omnicompetent minister up to which too many people have attempted to live... Ordained ministers [presbyters] therefore need to become aware of what it means to be part of a corporate body as well as to recognise their individual gifts, graces and skills.

In reviewing the development of the recent house-church

movement in the United Kingdom, David Harper of the Hallam Business School argued that it was effective because its leaders could motivate the laity. They do so not from a distant authoritarian position, but on a level with the people among whom they live and work. They don't perform for the congregation, but empower them to take part. Harper concluded:

> People are any organisation's most important resource, not only in their capacity to work and use their skills but also in their ability to be creative and use their ideas in problem-solving and decision-making. Motivation of the people in an organisation increases productivity and gets the job done. Motivation is voluntary and releases the E factors: excitement, enthusiasm, energy and effort. Within a church context, there may be a number of negative forces to overcome before individuals see that involvement and participation in the work of the church is actually their job and not just the leader's.

Church members in many traditional denominations today are excluded from participation in the mission of the church by their 'omnicompetent' ministers. Their ministers don't know how to motivate them or give them a vision of what might be. Their leaders don't involve them in a clearly defined mission strategy, or enable them to see that their witness can make a difference. Many church members can't take part because the omnicompetent one man band is playing all the instruments!

Church leaders can be so intent on doing things themselves that they have no time for empowering others. In my research of early church life in the New Towns of the 1960s and 70s I found a tragic prevalence of the one man band model of ministry. There was rarely any attempt to gather together a local leadership team, nor to identify potential new leaders among the incoming population. The clergy dominated the scene.

In one ecumenical church plant in a town which I have researched in detail, there were five clergy working together in one building. The committee minutes and reports show that from its very inception the policy of this ecumenical centre was completely clergy dominated. A team of five clerics representing different denominations was sent in to start a new church before the new population had arrived. Evidently, this meant that the new church's evolution became a reflection of their own ecumenical relationship and shared concepts of leadership. There was no opportunity for it to become what the local people might have wanted their church to be. One minister at the time commented: 'The existing team ministry is doing everything together – including Communion. But because of the nature of the project there is much to be arranged and a great deal of studying involved and this necessitates two staff meetings per week as well as the daily meeting for devotions.' While the professional clergy were busy developing their ecumenical relationships and holding their one man band rehearsals, the local folk were shut out. An early report admitted that it 'has been realised that a large ministerial team can too easily become an autocratic executive committee'.

In a dusty file I came across the following personal note from an expert observer sent in by one of the denominations to assess what was going on: 'I think that there is a great danger that the team make their decisions and are not open to other comments. The cost per annum of five men to learn to trust each other must be £10,000. How much to save the world?'

In July and August 1977 a comprehensive question-naire was completed by members of this church.

Responses to the question 'Have you any strong views about the way the Centre runs in general or any suggestions to make?' were few; but those who did dare to speak pleaded that 'the laity might share more in the decision-making processes'.

The church evidently registered this concern because a few months later it published a new Statement of Purpose, Aims and Objectives. This promised that 'the congregation shall be concerned to make full use of the talents and gifts of the laity'.

The Revd Richard Jones made a detailed assessment of this church's life and bemoaned the clerical domination: 'The result is that the congregation has not developed a pattern of life in which the laity take up a noticeably large share of leadership and responsibility. There are clear signs that some of the laity are sensitive to this.' The clergy leadership team was unable to empower others to take a full part in the life of the new centre. A recent Anglican incumbent observed: 'I think that there is a ministerial tendency to dominate. We have meetings where people say, "You don't listen," and it seems that some people think that the minister is the church. What have we done to make it feel like that? I've come across some church council minutes from the early days where there were four clergy and four church members present. That does seem highly questionable.'

These clergy in the northern town were all educated, white, male and middle class. This undoubtedly affected the development of church life there, and left little opportunity for the emergence of local working-class leaders in this predominantly blue-collar 'overspill' town.

A Methodist minister who is serving with this church looked back on the early models of leadership and told me: 'While the population is largely working class, the ministerial team reflected a middle-class culture. The local community possibly felt inadequate, and were unwilling to offer help because professional people were already filling the leadership roles.'

This one man band style of clerical leadership illustrates what can happen when local people are neither envisioned nor empowered. The abundant resources of local leadership, energy and commitment are simply shut out. Hundreds of churches are withering and dying because they are led by devotees of the one man band concept of ministry. The gifts and energies of local people have been pushed aside so that the leader can take the limelight. This is not a biblical model of leadership, and those who have trained generations of ministers to conform to such a model have done the church a grave disservice. Ultimately this style of leadership does not follow the Jesus model, for it speaks of personal power rather than sacrificial servanthood.

Empowerment of others

The hallmark of good leadership is not how well the leader plays all the instruments, but how well he or she conducts the orchestra. A detailed analysis of effective leadership characteristics in growing businesses concluded that, above all, effective leaders must be able to empower others: 'Visionaries create the conditions of trust and responsibility which empower subordinates to lead their bits of the enterprise and to feel ownership of its direction.' This ability to empower others results in further empowerment for the leader. Mintzberg posited that visionary leaders become part of an 'empowerment loop' – as well as empowering others, the leader is empowered by subordinates. The subordinates hand back trust, responsibility, support and applause, and this moulds the leader.

In a detailed examination of leadership styles in *The Harvard Business Review,* Peter Tannenbaum and Warren Schmidt produced a model of leadership styles which identified a range of leader behaviour ranging from the leader-centred approach to the group-centred approach; from the one man band to the conductor of an orchestra. At one extreme the leader 'decides and announces decisions', and at the other the leader gives the group 'as much freedom as he has to define the problem and decide on suitable courses of action'.

The strength of the participatory style of leadership is that it involves others in the work. Time and again in my own ministry I have discovered that where I provide opportunities for others to own aspects of a project they become deeply committed. Where I make space for them to invest their own creativity, they develop the project in ways I would never have imagined. When we all work together, the whole thing becomes much more fun.

One of the church's most urgent tasks is to stop expecting its leaders to fill a thousand diverse roles and to equip them to mobilise others to help get the job done. The theological colleges are far too committed to producing one man bands. They are simply not training future leaders to envision, enthuse and empower others to do the work that God is calling them to do.

Henry Mintzberg has suggested that successful chief executives rely more on 'feel' and intuition than systematic reasoning. They 'synthesise' rather than 'analyse', and they know, intuitively, more than they can communicate. They revel in ambiguity and dislike regularity. He concludes that creative strategy needs 'right brain thinking' which usually comes from one person. As I visit different theological colleges I do not recognise a commitment to raising up this style of future church leader.

In *Planting Tomorrow's Churches Today*, Stuart Christine looked at six failed Baptist church plants. The prime cause of failure was identified as inadequate leadership. He went on to identify the most important qualities of a church-plant leader, and one of the most significant was: 'An ability to inspire others to catch the vision.'

While traditional styles of ministerial training look to the production of scholars, preachers and theologians, the church's greatest need is to find leaders who can inspire others to catch a vision. The church needs more missionary entrepreneurs! These are not men and women who will parade their scholarship in a weekly one man band performance; these are people who know how to release others in the gifts they have. This is not a ministry of personal power but of corporate empowerment.

One of the most effective visionary leaders I know is the Revd John Ed Mathison of Frazier Memorial United Church in Montgomery, Alabama. It is a church which has seen spectacular growth, and it is built on one simple principle: every member in ministry.

Mathison argues that 'our significance in life comes from being called by God for ministry. Since we were nothing when God called us, this gives us no reason to boast for our being called by God. We are not called because of what we have done. We find our significance in the fact that God initiates the call to us and we respond in service.' Mathison has proved beyond doubt that motivation of the laity is a major key to church growth. As each church member begins to grasp a vision, they begin to find their part in fulfilling it. He writes:

This concept has far-reaching implications for the church staff. Staff members of a church should never be hired to do ministry, but to train laity to do ministry. This concept multiplies the avenues of ministry for the church. If a church hires one person to do youth ministry, that person would be limited in his/her opportunity for outreach. But, if that person then trains thirty lay people who have gifts in the area of youth ministry, then look how far-reaching that youth ministry can be through the congregation.

The visionary leader

J. P. Kolter of Harvard Business School makes a clear distinction in *The Leadership Factor* between leadership and management. Leadership has vision, communicates vision and has the ability to get people to follow. Such leaders can recruit and motivate people to work to the vision by inspiring and directing them. This is different from the management function which ensures an efficient and effective use of resources. Managers have an ability to organise and administrate and are essential, but they represent something different from leadership.

The magazine *Bottom Line Personnel* interviewed management consultant Warren Bennis about the essential qualities for leadership. He made it clear that leaders are very different animals from managers:

Managers administer; leaders innovate. Managers are system focused; leaders are people focused. Managers rely on control; leaders rely on trust. Managers must watch the bottom line; leaders must watch the horizon. The best leaders combine a concern for details with a grasp of the big picture. They also have moved beyond the command-and-control model of leading to a more flexible, empowering, energising style that makes people feel valued and liberated to take risks.

For generations, our theological colleges have been turning out one man bands – high achievers and polished performers who can preach, administrate, manage and counsel. In every role they perform, they parade their own abilities, but they do not develop the gifts of others. They rarely demonstrate the 'flexible, empowering, energising style that makes people feel valued' much commended by Bennis. They play many instruments but cannot conduct an orchestra, for they lack visionary leadership.

Many churches in the United States have begun to recognise the crucial importance of vision for their future growth and development. Joe Harding and Ralph Mohney's popular church programme called 'Vision 2000' made the point:

> A church with vision that is constantly affirmed and lifted up will always be an exciting, dynamic, energizing centre of hope. These congregations tend to be Great Commission centred, rather than self-centred. Their attitude tends to be, 'We cannot do it all, but we can do something.' Visionary congregations experience the life of faith as an inspiring journey, rather than a depressing obligation. There is a joyful contagion about these congregations. This posture of forward-leaning receptivity positions people to receive new visions that call forth new approaches to previously unseen needs.

Where is this vision to be found? It must come from the emerging generation of new leaders who must be set free to dream new dreams. Schon, in his paper, 'Champions for Radical New Invention', suggested that one way of helping institutions to introduce innovative patterns of work lies in the development of 'champions' for new ideas:

> The champion must be a man (or woman) willing to put him(her)self on the line for an idea of doubtful success. He is

willing to fail but he is capable of using any and every means of informal ways and pressure to succeed. No ordinary involvement with a new idea provides the energy required to cope with the indifference and resistance that major technical change requires. It is characteristic of champions of new developments that they identify with the idea as their own, and with its promotion as a cause, to a degree that goes far beyond the requirements of their job.

We need more envisioners and fewer one man bands. We need leaders whose role is to dream a dream, and to involve others in the creation of a strategy to fulfil it. The church needs leaders who do not have an inbred aversion to innovation and change, but who constantly strive to see how things can be done better. Dr Bill Richardson of Hallam University Business School defines a visionary leader:

> The visionary makes 'mental leaps' which take 'what is now' into 'what could or should be'. This 'imagining', however, is not done in a void. Rather, it draws from a deep understanding of what already is – it is grounded in experience of the industry or profession in which the visionary's new approach is to prove successful. The visions of successful leaders are usually built on thousands of hours of experience in a particular profession or industry and a similarly massive amount of time spent mulling over the challenges being faced therein.

Father Theodore Hersburg, former President of Notre Dame University, stated: 'The very essence of leadership is that you have to have a vision. It has got to be a vision you can articulate clearly and forcefully on every occasion. You can't blow an uncertain trumpet.'

In the church of the new millennium we need leaders who don't play in one man bands. They prefer to create beautiful symphonies. They hear new harmonies and communicate the wonder of the music to those who have never heard it. They don't want to perform the music on their own; they want to share the joy of creativity with all the other players.

This kind of visionary leader can draw together a mighty orchestra with each player committed to their task. He is the facilitator, not the performer. His greatest thrill is to see the orchestra playing in perfect harmony. When this is accomplished he steps back into the shadows and knows that the vision is fulfilled, the dream has come true.

Christian leaders must be encouraged to develop personal vision, and taught how to impart this vision to others. In four years of theological education I never heard anything about vision or empowerment. The emphasis was on making me a better one man band rather than the effective leader of a strong orchestra.

Kenneth Cracknell, President Emeritus of Cambridge Theological Federation and Research Professor at Brite Divinity School in Texas, admitted that mid-nineteenth-century theological education contained little missiological relevance. His research about the feelings of students at that time was very revealing:

> So far as the theological lectures of the College were concerned... they created within him a revulsion of feeling against the system of lecturing then in vogue, which consisted of repeating over again to successive groups of students lectures which had never had much contact with reality and had certainly never grown beyond their first inception.

More than a century later many contemporary theological students feel just the same. In 1991 a report entitled 'Ministerial Training Policy' in the Methodist Church stated the need for training to be rooted in an all-pervasive sense of mission, seeking to create a better understanding of ourselves and the world in the light of Christ's ministry to the world. Training should equip ministers with skills in interpreting social context and Christian tradition, to enable them to be agents of change and instruments of the Kingdom of God.

This is all very well in theory, but I've not seen much of it in my visits to theological colleges of various traditions in recent years. The traditional models of equipping the one man band still prevail. When I suggested that a dynamic young Christian leader needed to be trained as a church planter, the Methodist official responsible for theological education suggested that I had better 'send him to the Baptists'!

The traditional denominations need to call hundreds of young Christians with characteristics of visionary leadership into the church's ministry. We need to give them a new freedom to experiment and innovate, and to encourage them to hear new music and to gather new orchestras. They must be free to make mistakes, to learn and to experiment.

The missionary entrepreneur

In 'The Making of Ministry', a discussion paper published by the Methodist Church in 1996, three questions were posed: 'What does God require the Church to be and do as it enters the twenty-first century? What type of members and, in particular, leaders will there be in such a Church? What forms of training will be needed to equip and support such a variety of ministries and roles?' The report goes on to suggest that 'the Spirit is given to the whole Church and only then focused in individual members in the form of particular gifts, abilities and responsibilities. Moreover these particular gifts are given not for the aggrandisement of the individuals who receive them, but for the benefit of the Church and the world in whose service they are to use them.'

I would suggest that one of the most urgent gifts to be identified, supported and resourced is the gift of the entrepreneur in mission. The church desperately needs leaders who can pioneer new work, develop new congregations and undertake dynamic experiments in contemporary mission. In a time of such appalling decline and ineffectiveness, the church must find new ways of doing mission, which is its core business.

Management supremos Rothwell and Zegveld suggested that the need to promote entrepreneurship and to stimulate innovation and maintain growth has been recognised by many corporations for some time. A survey conducted in the 1970s suggested that one in four of the thousand largest American corporations had established formal or informal entrepreneurship programmes designed to facilitate entrepreneurial activity.

If only one in four churches had a cleric who was part of an entrepreneurship programme. If only one in four churches freed up its personnel to engage in visionary new ventures. If only one in four churches allowed its leaders to experiment in mission within secular culture. If only one in four local congregations didn't demand a one man band but allowed its leader to conduct the orchestra. There is nothing new in this, for it is simply a rediscovery of the role of the missionary apostle found in the ministries of people like Peter and Paul.

My hope is that the new visionary leaders will involve others in the fulfilment of their vision. They will hear a richer harmony and encourage others to take their part in creating it. An air of creativity and excitement will grow and grow until everyone is pushing themselves to the limit. No cost will be too great, no effort too demanding, no sacrifice too painful, for everyone will be working to see the same dream come true: the kingdom of God come on earth. We must begin to introduce radical forms of leadership into local congregations, and to enable them to release leaders for mission instead of keeping them preoccupied with maintenance.

Ultimately, however, the true leader will be equipped by God. Samuel Chadwick, the founder of Cliff College, wrote in 1932: 'A ministry that is College-trained but not Spirit-filled works no miracles.' The church of the new millennium needs leaders who are visionaries; leaders who are motivators; leaders who are evangelists. But above all it needs leaders who are full to overflowing with the power of the Holy Spirit.

DISCUSSION: A VISION FOR LEADERSHIP

Icebreaker

Cut out newspaper pictures of leaders of nations, governments and industry.

What does the world look for in a leader?

What makes a leader truly great?

Bible base

Read together Matthew 20:20–28.

Discussion questions

- What were the qualities Jesus expected to find in the leaders of the kingdom?
- Why are such qualities still important today?
- Why were Wesley's leaders so effective when their Anglican counterparts were so detached from the new communities?
- Have you ever known what it is like to be motivated by a leader? Describe the experience.
- Describe a church with a one man band and a church with a fully motivated congregation. What would be the major differences? Which would you prefer to belong to?
- Do you agree with the 'every member in ministry' concept?
- If so, how can we develop church life to accommodate it?
- How can the church begin to identify visionary leaders?
- How best can they be trained and equipped?
- Where would you use such people in the life of the church?
- What is a missionary entrepreneur?
- Are such people valued in the life of the church today?
- If not, why not?

(Feel free to range over the questions in any order. It's not crucial to answer them all!)

CHAPTER 6

A Vision for the Church

A small cluster of elderly church members stood silently and watched as the crane moved to and fro. The huge metal ball suspended from the gantry began to swing and as it gained momentum it drew closer to the wall. Then, quite suddenly, there was a deafening crash and it slammed through the masonry. Again and again the engine roared and the ball plunged through the brickwork. Bricks rained down, dust filled the air like morning mist and the splintered rafters hung precariously from the half-demolished roof.

The chapel was coming down. Generations had worshipped there, and as I saw it turn to rubble I was deeply moved. I thought of the countless people who had met within those walls to sing their praises, mourn their dead and bless their newborn. It was the end of an era.

Deep in the pile of debris one of the demolition crew found a glass bottle. Inside there was a letter from the congregation which had built the chapel nearly a century before. As I read the faded papers I wondered how they would have felt about the demolition of their chapel. I wanted to tell them that this demolition wasn't a sign of defeat but of the church moving on. The demise of their

119

building was to make way for new dimensions in worship and new directions in mission.

Many aspects of the church's life will have to be demolished to make way for the church of the new millennium. Treasured traditions and religious cultures must be swept away to make room for what is to come. For some of us, it will be heartbreaking to watch. We must redraw our denominational map to respond to Wesley's slogan 'Go to those who need you most'; not to the large lush suburban churches, but to the people groups in our society who have no witness and no chance of hearing the good news.

Our strategy must be to plant small cell groups where interpersonal relationships can be strong, each individual's contribution valued, and a fellowship of corporate strength developed. We must provide an alternative to the cold, unfriendly and lonely society where the individual feels devalued, and where the acquisition of things has become more important than the development of individual potential.

Several years ago the District Superintendent of the Philippine Methodist Church unveiled a plan to begin a new work to 'awake the sleeping giant'. He targeted four Southern Tagalog provinces where there were no Methodist churches, and embarked on an ambitious programme of church planting using evangelists. He twinned unchurched areas with existing congregations. After many years of stagnation and membership decline, the Methodist Church in the Philippines now reports a massive 10 per cent annual growth rate. What happened in the Philippines can happen in the denominational churches here in Britain. If the church is to engage in effective mission it must move beyond the friendship networks of its church members to begin a new work in the secular world.

Robert Currie, writing in *Churches and Churchgoers,* declared: 'If a church is to grow as fast as the population it must be able to recruit an expanding constituency; and if it is to grow at all, it must, given wastage, be able to recruit persons other than its own members' children.' This suggests that evangelism should have a far higher priority and a far more important profile in the Methodist Church than it does at present.

In *The Testing of the Churches*, Rupert Davies observed:

> Rightly or wrongly, the Methodist Church as a whole in the last three decades has swung from a policy of evangelism conceived as a self-justifying and self-contained activity, to one of including it in its total mission. It has, of course, not disowned the narrower and more intense forms of evangelism, but it has tended to leave them to certain vigorous groups within itself and often...too often?...to evangelists from overseas, such as Billy Graham.

It could be argued that the encompassing of evangelism in the total mission of the church has led to a downgrading of its importance, and that there have been periods in the last thirty years in which evangelistic activity has been marginalised, discredited and even ridiculed.

If the church is to address the needs of the secular society it wishes to reach, then it must take the task of evangelism much more seriously. It is when the leaders of our denominations undertake a personal commitment to evangelism, and when church ministers take the reality of the secular society seriously that we might see the mobilisation of the laity into a wave of proclamation, service and witness which will challenge the agnosticism of the secular society.

The mission to secular society is the responsibility of every Christian, and is not just the domain of missiologists or evangelists. There is a massive resource of people waiting to be released in personal and lifestyle evangelism. People who, at present, are too engrossed in 'playing church' to address the challenge of the present age. At a time when the church worldwide is growing at its fastest ever rate, it is frustrating to be part of a church where decline is apparent on every side.

The mainline churches of the United Kingdom have not responded to the changing society which they are called to serve. Many leaders and churchgoers seem blissfully unaware of these changes. It is so easy for Christians to become embroiled in church life and cocooned against the secular world. Indeed, for some, the church can even be a refuge from the world where 'The storm may roar without me...but nothing changes here.'

There seems an underlying assumption in the institutions of our churches that our models of church life, worship, ministry and mission are appropriate for the present. Nothing could be further from the truth. The church needs to turn from its selfish preoccupation with maintenance, and to serve the society in which it is based. We need to identify unreached peoples within our communities. We need to determine a strategy for incarnational mission among them. We need to see service and caring as implicit in our mission, creating means to meet local needs, and this may even necessitate relocating to where people are. We need to develop forms of communication and styles of worship which are culturally relevant to the groups identified.

Once the church in Britain stops pretending that Britain is a Christian country and moves from being an establishment to being a missionary movement, I believe that we will know that the secular fields really are white unto harvest.

I do not claim to predict what shape the church will take, or to prophesy the future. My ideas are a combination of hope, guesswork and possibilities. There are present trends which, if projected forward, give us a clue as to what might be, and there are personal hopes which I pray will one day be fulfilled.

If this book triggers a debate and helps us to see the possibilities which God has set before us it will have achieved its purpose. The future of the church can sometimes seem bewildering, but there is a way out of the maze, and God can see it. If we ask him, he will surely show us what to do.

Worship

Much of the institutional church will have to disappear to make way for the new church. Many tears will be shed as power structures are dismantled and hallowed traditions demolished. Familiar denominational systems will disappear as new ways of networking and systems of authority develop. Hierarchies which have hindered change and innovation will collapse under the growing pressure of their financial difficulties.

New young leaders will envision the church and make it more relevant and Jesus-centred. Those of us who have survived a generation of decline, disillusionment and despair will see things that we hardly even dared to hope for.

In the world of today people are the focus of everything. They tame the elements, explore the universe, store knowledge and control their own destiny. It is little wonder that many churchgoers struggle when they try to approach the Almighty, and long for services to be more entertaining and enjoyable. Sadly, they haven't really understood what spirituality is.

The church of the new millennium will recognise society's growing hunger for a spirituality which works – a need already expressed everywhere from the Body Shop to New Age music and from ecological work-groups to T'ai Chi.

Worship in the church of the new millennium will change to fit the shape of the culture in which it finds itself. It will move on fast and become increasingly relevant to the society of the new millennium. Worship is a living form like art, and it will develop in revolutionary ways.

The Bible doesn't teach that services should be traditional, and when churchgoers advocate a return to traditional worship it is hard to know which tradition they are referring to. Are they appealing to the Jewish tradition of worship, which so influenced the development of Christianity? In the years after the Exile there was a growing need to worship at home. Ceremonies and prayers within the ongoing life of the family were often the most important expressions of worship. Or are they thinking of the early church tradition, when Christians met daily in the Temple, shared meals together and lived in eager anticipation of the return of Jesus? Or perhaps they are looking to the great fathers of the early church – Justin Martyr, Tertullian and Cyprian – who each founded different strands of liturgical tradition? Or maybe their definitive kind of worship goes back to Constantine. For after his conversion the Christian church was recognised by the State for the first time, the homely services disappeared and large gathered congregations began to rely on clerical leadership in their worship.

Some look to the Eastern traditions from Jerusalem and Antioch, others to the worship of Rome and the West. Some revere the worship of the Middle Ages, when services were read by clergy and the congregation looked on as silent spectators. Others respect the Reformation with its simple language, bare sanctuaries, prominent preaching and extemporary prayers.

Many twentieth-century Christians look back to the hymns of Wesley, the gospel songs of Sankey, the brass bands of Booth, or the praise music of Kendrick. Or they imagine that definitive worship is to be found at Spring Harvest or Easter People. The church of the new millennium, however, will draw from a much wider spectrum of worship resources. It will be all the richer because it taps into such a diverse range of traditions.

Post-modernism is a rediscovery of roots, and the church will come to appreciate its heritage and connect with the riches of its ancient worship culture. There will be a growth of interest in traditional liturgy, ancient prayers, the beauty of silence and the flickering aura of candlelight.

Dr Eddie Gibbs, formerly a lecturer in church planting at the Fuller School of World Mission, has returned to pastoral ministry as a curate in the parish with the world's most salubrious postcode: Beverley Hills 902101. He points out that his parishioners, who are the stars of the movie industry and the culture shapers of America, are looking for spiritual roots and for time to reflect and be still. He questions whether much of our busy contemporary worship is relevant to the newly emerging post-modern culture. The church of the new millennium will recognise that its worship must be closely connected to the rich and diverse heritage of its ancient past.

Sir John Betjeman spoke for many when he wrote:

All I can say is that with age I find myself enjoying more and more the words and rhythms of the Book of Common Prayer. Apart from their meaning, they sound right and they are not talking down to us by being matey, and where they're a bit vague and archaic, that makes them grand and historic. The words give me time to meditate and pray; they are so familiar, they are like my birthplace, and I don't want them pulled down.

A church without a sense of the past has no roots, but if it has no sense of tomorrow it will have no future. A church can't live on tradition and it will not survive if it lets the past dominate. A Commission of the World Council of Churches on worship concluded: 'Faithfulness to tradition requires therefore the utmost sensitivity – to the claims of God who does not change and to the needs of men and women who are always changing.' The church's task is to take hold of the past with one hand and the future with the other, and to shape its worship within the creative tension of the present.

The new church will recognise that good worship is connected to real life. It is a living form that must be free to develop. We can only guess what kind of media might be used, what the music will be like or what form the services will take, but these forms are only a means to an end, not an end in themselves. Those who believe that the worship band and the five-line chorus are the definitive form of contemporary worship must beware. Our world is changing fast, and the day is not far distant when the worship group will seem as culturally peculiar as the brass band.

Many will rediscover the lost art of 'practising the presence of God'. They will find a new awareness of the Holy Spirit and come to prayer with a new hunger for the living God. They will pray with mind and spirit and echo Paul's experience when he wrote: 'So what shall I do? I will pray with my spirit, but I will also pray with my mind' (1 Cor 14:15). Worship will both renew and transform.

The church's rich heritage of liturgy will be rediscovered with its oft-repeated words full of meaning. Music will take greater prominence and will become integral to the prayer experience. Prayer through music will be commonplace, be it sung Evensong, jazz mass, folk celebration or classic meditation.

The new churches will rediscover art, from the iconography of the East to the statues of Rome, and they will develop their own contemporary spirituality through it. Frequently changing displays, pictures, posters and banners will become a growing inspiration for prayer as the churches learn how to use the visual arts as a means and not an end.

Gifts of healing will be given to the body of Christ and the church will draw on them more and more. It will demonstrate that true power lies not in massage, aromatherapy or T'ai Chi, but in the anointing of oil and the promises of God. The laying on of hands will symbolise corporate faith and demonstrate the church's ongoing ministry of wholeness. The gift of healing will come to prominence as many rediscover Christ's healing power.

The core activity of the church will be worship, and the new church will learn how to lead a mortal people to an immortal God. Worship will become an attitude which is present all week, and corporate worship will be the culmination of a daily life of praise. The church of the new millennium will teach that the whole of life is worship, not just an hour on Sundays. There will be no great divide between sacred and secular, Sunday and Monday. All that God's people are, all that they do, and all that they have will be their daily offering.

The ancient community of Qumran (where the Dead Sea Scrolls were discovered) taught that worship is part of everyday life. Manual 10 in the Qumran Rule of Discipline says: 'As long as I live it shall be a rule engraved on my tongue, to bring praise like a fruit for an offering and my lips as a sacrificial gift.'

Time and again the writers of the Psalms urged their readers to make praise a way of life. King David wrote: 'I will bless the Lord at all times: his praise shall continually be in my mouth' (Ps 34:1, AV). In Psalm 113 we read: 'From the rising of the sun unto the going down of the same the Lord's name is to be praised' (Ps 113:3, AV).

Worship will be about shopping in the supermarket and driving on congested roads. It will flow from family relationships and from caring for awkward colleagues. It will come out of the frustration of difficult work and the joy of a job well done. It will celebrate the presence of God in the nitty-gritty of everyday routine. Worship will be life itself. 'Whatever you do, whether in word or deed,' wrote Paul, 'do it all in the name of the Lord Jesus, giving thanks to God the Father through him' (Col 3:17). The quality of people's worship will flow from the quality of their lives. Worship will be what they take to church, not what they go to receive. It will become a lifestyle of sacrifice, not an opportunity to get blessed.

They will rediscover the joy of family worship, which Orthodox Jews still experience each Friday evening on the eve of Sabbath, and find that even social occasions can flow seamlessly into worship. Work and worship will be one, with work an expression of people's love for God. Sacred and secular will be joined, and they will worship less in the sanctuary and more in the world. Services in the home, the work-place and the community will predominate, and worship in the church will diminish.

This church will worship in the same power which moved over the waters at creation and which brought divine order from the chaos. It is a power of limitless reserves, with signs and wonders which follow in his refreshing flow.

Community

The church of the new millennium will understand that its communal life is a sign of the kingdom of God. The church will become the antidote for the fragmentation of the family and the breakdown of human relationships. It will work to counter the lonely isolation in which countless millions will live their lives. It will celebrate the contribution of all. Congregations will express the kingdom in real relationships which echo God's adoptive love. They will discover that worship flows from the richness of their communal life, and churches will not consist of clubs and meetings but networks of deep relationships.

Churches will be villages that are the focus of deep belonging. They will recognise that the world is not looking for an organisation to join but a community to be part of. The cell groups of the church won't refuse those who have no ticket of membership or certificate of baptism, but will welcome all who are fellow travellers on the road of faith to join them – each one helping the other towards the goal of holiness.

The church of the new millennium will recognise the diversity of worship styles, and affirm all which ring true with the Bible. The woman of Samaria asked Jesus if God should be worshipped at the holy place in Samaria or in Jerusalem. She wanted to know if Samaritan culture worship was as acceptable to the Lord as Jerusalem style worship. But Jesus made it clear that location was irrelevant: 'It's who you are and the way you live that count before God. Your worship must engage your spirit in the pursuit of truth. That's the kind of people the Father is out looking for: those who are simply and honestly *themselves* before him in their worship. God is sheer being itself – Spirit. Those who worship him must do it out of their very being, their spirits, their true selves, in adoration' (Jn 4:23–24, *The Message*). The motivating power of the Holy Spirit will move through simple choruses and classic hymns. He will empower ancient liturgies and the faltering prayers of children. He will move through the joy of dance and the solemnity of the Requiem.

Post-modern society will not be one mass culture but a celebration of many cultures. It will not consist of one kind of people, but many different people groups. Life will not become more uniform, but more diverse. The church, through its multitude of cell groups, will create the space for this rich diversity to find expression within its worship life, and each village will be united through the all-encompassing love of God. Uniformity will disappear as different groups enjoy the worship which most expresses who they are. The cell groups may be large or small, but each will rejoice in the promise of Jesus that 'where two or three come together in my name, I am there with them'.

There will be no room for passengers in the new church, for each cell will demand a deep commitment to its fellowship life. Clusters of the cells will form each Christian village, and from time to time the whole community will gather to celebrate the joy of loving Jesus and the rich diversity of their belonging.

Relevance

The church in the new millennium will be a radical expression of the kingdom. It will speak to the conscience of the world and challenge its destructive inclinations. It will live simply, question consumerism and hedonism and oppose the status quo. It will pioneer new ethical standards for the world and move strongly in the prophetic gift of the Holy Spirit.

Prophetic preaching will be an integral part of this church's ministry and lifestyle. Preaching is a vital ministry and many churches have grown lazy in their administration of it. Not only have we forced preachers to serve in situations which were clearly inappropriate, but we have made them preach themselves dry. Some preachers have laboured to serve the same unappreciative congregation for year upon year, and have become drained as a result.

It is said that 23 per cent of the population do not read a newspaper at all, and that 22 per cent have never read a book. Yet congregations are often expected to use three different books during a one-hour service. The language of the pulpit often reflects that of the quality newspapers, but 19 per cent read the *Sun* and 18 per cent read the *Mirror.* Preachers in the new church will learn how to communicate. Those responsible for preaching will learn what television chief, Sir Charles Curran, once described as 'an ability to convince the audience of their wish to expose themselves to what we want to say'. Preachers will not expect their listeners to understand 'Godspeak', to struggle with alien concepts, to comprehend religious norms or to relate to archaic language. They will begin to speak the language of the people.

Philip Hawthorn wrote: 'Just as ordinary people felt excluded by the Latin liturgy in the Middle Ages, so many people today feel excluded by the church's forbidding message buried in strange rituals and religious language. If God cares for all people then Christians must find ways to get out of their ghettos and into the modern market place.' The church of the new millennium will discover that preaching is storytelling. Communication in a post-modern society will no longer be a diatribe of opinions, hypotheses and dogma. Good stories will grip the listeners' attention and communicate deep meanings for their lives.

Jesus' style was pithy, uncluttered and poignant. He did not use an introduction, three points and a conclusion, or reason his audience to sleep. He didn't need to build a complex structure of argument to get his point across. What he said made sense. Jesus communicated his message with urgency for the time was near and the kingdom was at hand. He communicated with authority and expected an immediate response.

Every preacher in the new church will be preaching for response, for they will be working under a divine commission and there won't be much time left. Preachers will be exponents of our choices and demand verdicts from those who listen.

Jesus was always relevant. He didn't focus on religion, but on people's everyday fears and failings. In some contexts preaching and Christian communication will major on apologetics, and will give a reasoned intellectual defence of the faith that is within us. Science, philosophy, psychology and ethics will be debated in the arena of Christian understanding. Steve Chalke, writing in *For Such a Time as This*, declared:

> For much of the time, we have effectively turned the gospel into something with which the majority of people cannot identify. One television producer put it to me this way: 'You evangelicals are always trying to answer Question 17 when we are not even sure what Question no. 1 is yet. In fact, some of you are worse than the politicians. It makes absolutely no difference what our question is, you always tell us what you want us to hear anyway.'

The source of the preachers' authority will not lie in their political opinions, their true life experiences or their prejudices. It will lie deep within the word of God. Sermons without a biblical context will be discredited.

Paul wrote: 'The appeal we make to you is not based on error or impure motives, nor do we try to trick anyone. Instead, we always speak as God wants us to, because he approved us and entrusted the Good News to us. We do not try to please men, but to please God, who tests our motives' (1 Thess 2:3–4, TEV).

The church of the new millennium will recognise that the work of preaching is less to do with delivery and style, and more to do with the life of the one who preaches. Bishop Quayle summed it up when he wrote:

> The elemental business in preaching is not with the preaching, but with the preacher. It is no trouble to preach, but a vast trouble to construct a preacher. What then, in the light of this, is the task of the preacher? Mainly this, the amassing of a great soul so as to have something worthwhile to give – the sermon is the preacher up to date.

The arts

The church of the new millennium will develop the use of the arts in its worship, celebration, participation and communication. It will speak in the vernacular of the CD-ROM generation, and drama will be more important than ever. Drama has been part of Christian worship since the tenth century when the liturgy itself began to make use of dialogue, movement, gestures, impersonation, role-play and symbolism. A prime example is found in the tenth-century book *Concordia Regularis,* which detailed a religious mime to be performed by the monks.

By the twelfth century, liturgical drama was becoming popular. Plays linked to Easter and Christmas were frequently performed. One drama involved Rachel's lamenting the death of the 'Innocents' in the Christmas story, and another was about the three kings from the East. Thomas Aquinas, by the direction of the Pope, developed an office for the festival of Corpus Christi in about 1264. Within fifty years this had become a popular festival, with religious processions a central part of the festivities.

By the fourteenth century, a more extempore form of drama had evolved. The Mystery plays were dramatic presentations about Creation, the Annunciation, the Passion, the Ascension and the Last Judgement. The words of the plays were expanded, utilising the language and dialect of the people, and with interpolations from non-biblical characters. Around this time the laity replaced the clergy as the actors, craft guilds taking on the responsibility for the production, fishmongers producing Jonah and carpenters Noah's Ark!

A primitive form of street theatre developed around these processions. These were based on history, from the Fall of Lucifer to the Last Judgement, and different versions featured between twenty-five and fifty short plays. They were presented in religious centres such as cathedral cities. The Chester cycle of plays was founded in 1328, and similar productions began in York in 1377 and Coventry in 1392. Many local parish churches copied the idea on a smaller scale. These cycles were major events and involved the whole community.

Next came the Morality plays which developed in the fifteenth century. They depicted the story of man's journey from birth to the grave. At the heart of the Morality play was man's choice between right and wrong. Characters in the Morality plays were personifications of good and evil, vice and virtue.

R. A. Banks, in his historic view of fifteenth- and early sixteenth-century Morality plays, noted: 'Preaching or didacticism seems fundamentally the main purpose of such plays; allegory is merely the manner used to convey the message.'

Over the centuries, therefore, the church has used drama as an integral part of its communication. Yet today it is often relegated to special guest services or entrusted to those with little skill or expertise. The church of the new millennium will put drama back on centre-stage.

Drama is storytelling brought up to date. David Hornbrook, a drama education expert, noted: 'Today, the pervasive presence of television in modern society has meant that we now have constant access to drama in ways never before possible. Drama has become built into the rhythms of our everyday lives, serving to confirm and reassure in a world in which active intervention in public life has come for many to seem futile and meaningless.'

In the new church drama will be seen as a prime means of effective communication. Actor Nigel Forde wrote: 'Prophetic theatre is theatre which clarifies the word of God at a particular time; Evangelistic theatre is that which clarifies the gospel in particular; Didactic theatre – in this context – clarifies the teaching of the Bible, and Entertaining theatre is based on the nature of humankind and creation.'

Increasingly, educationalists are discovering that drama is not an isolated subject but something at the heart of effective communication. Drama teachers are working across the subject base in order to bring ideas about geography, history, art and religion to life. Drama educationalist Betty Jane Wagner explains: 'If we think of any material stored in books as an unpalatable beef bouillon cube, then some means must be found for releasing this dense mass into a savoury broth of human experience. In educational circles, this message has been called code-cracking, breaking the code so the message can be read.'

The primary role of drama in proclamation, therefore, will not be to hammer home the message but to grab the audience's attention, to entertain, to tell stories, to raise questions, to hold up a mirror to human experience and to question people's presuppositions, so that the preacher has a listening audience waiting to make a connection. Gordon and Ronnie Lamont wrote:

> We use drama quite naturally as a way of helping us to make sense of our lives, of understanding God and his world. This is not some trendy add-on to our Christianity, it is right there at the heart of our faith. We follow the example of Jesus who opened up difficult questions about God and his kingdom by inviting his hearers into an 'as if' world.

Drama is at its most useful when the viewers, empathising with the characters, recognise some situation, some aspect of their lives or some burning question and, through this process of recognition, become riveted to the plot and open to the message. David Hornbrook explains: 'We may therefore regard dramatic art not so much as another way of knowing, but rather as a way of participating in dramatic conversations which can lead to new perceptions, to us making better sense of things.'

The church of the new millennium will discover exciting ways of communicating its message and of making the gospel understandable and relevant to a television generation. The use of modern media in evangelism will not be seen as religious entertainment or compromise with the world, just effective communication.

The arts will not change or cheapen the gospel, nor will they replace preaching; they will complement it. The language of film, music, drama, poetry and dance will be the vernacular of the new generation, and the church will learn how to speak it, and speak it fluently.

Hope

The church of the new millennium will cease to be denominational, and the age-old games of ecclesiastical rivalry will finally end. M. Crozier, in *Comparing Structures and Comparing Games,* observed: 'An organization can be considered as a set of games, more or less explicitly defined, between groups of partners who have to play with each other. These games are played according to some informal rules which cannot be easily predicted from the prescribed roles of the formal structure.'

Under the continuing pressure of secularisation and a grass-roots desire to work together, the old games of denominational churchmanship will end, and a new season of united action will begin. New ways of working together will not flow out of new ecumenical formulae, but out of deep relationships within the family of God.

J. Child, in *The Contribution of Organization Structure,* identifies various examples where there is a breakdown of working relationships among organisations. The writer concludes:

There may be conflict and a lack of co-ordination because there are conflicting goals which have not been structured into a single set of objectives and priorities. People are acting at cross-purposes. They may, for example, be put under pressure to follow departmental priorities at the expense of project goals. People are working out of step with each other because they are not brought together into teams or because mechanisms for liaison have not been laid down.

The old denominational church structures, with their ongoing conflict, lack of co-ordination and conflicting goals, will disappear. Teams for local action and mission will be formed which help people to keep in step with each other. New local networks of Christians will develop, each one bringing something of the richness of their own tradition with them. Attempts to merge the churches into one bland pan-Protestant mix will be resisted. Each cell in the Christian village will retain distinctives from its denominational heritage, but the old days of rivalry will have gone for ever. There will be more crucial problems to solve.

Some believe that the new millennium will bring growing social chaos, a further breakdown of law and order, extensive ecological destruction and the disintegration of normal family relationships. They say that the future is bleak, if, indeed, there is a future at all.

No matter what the future holds, broken bread and poured wine will continue to be the focus of the church's hope, a sign of God's providential care, and a symbol that one day the journey will be over and his people will see him face to face. The new church will consist of people who know the end of the story, who have read the last page of history and who declare the victory of Jesus. They will live in the certainty of his coming kingdom and will anticipate the joy of meeting him face to face. 'All the angels were standing around the throne and around the elders and the four living creatures. They fell down on their faces before the throne and worshipped God, saying: "Amen! Praise and glory and wisdom and thanks and honour and power and strength be to our God for ever and ever. Amen!"' (Rev 7:11–12).

Which way for the church, then? The future begins now; and the work of shaping what the church will be starts here. Let us dream a dream, create a strategy and roll up our sleeves. There is much to be done....

DISCUSSION: A VISION FOR THE CHURCH

Icebreaker

Give each member of the group a polystyrene cup (not plastic) and ask them to do with it what they would like to see God do with the church in the new millennium.

Bible base

Read Revelation 7:9–17.
  What is the church?
  What will it be?

Discussion questions

- What is worship, and why do we do it?
- Which traditions of worship does your church draw on?
- How can worship become more a part of our ordinary lives?
- How does the breakdown of community life affect the people you know?
- How can the church become a kingdom community?
- What kind of things should the church be saying to the world?
- How can we say them so that they will be heard?
- Why are the arts important in the life of the church?

- How, practically, can we involve more people in creativity in the life of the church?
- How do you see the future of the church?
- What is your greatest fear and your greatest hope for the church?

(Feel free to discuss the questions in any order, and don't feel that you have to discuss them all!)

Papers, Reports and Interviews

'Beyond the Fringes'. Methodist Church Home Mission Report, 1996.

'Bold to Say'. Methodist Church Home Mission Report 118, 1974.

'British Politics and Society from Walpole to Pitt 1742–1789'. Ed. Jeremy Black. (Macmillan Education Ltd, 1990) p216.

'Called to Love and Praise'. The Methodist Church Faith and Order Committee Report to Conference, 1995.

'Called to Share'. Methodist Church Home Mission Report 117, 1973.

'Drift from the Churches – Secondary School Pupils' Attitudes towards Christianity'. *British Journal of Religious Education* (Vol II).

'Early Methodist Preachers'. Vol VI, p267.

'English People in the Eighteenth Century'. (Longman Green and Co, 1956) p275.

'Evangelical Strategy in the New Towns'. Report by the Evangelical Alliance, 1971.

'Going for Growth in a Christian Setting'. Paper submitted to 'Managing in an Enterprise Context' for Hallam University Business School, 1994, p8.

'Landmarc'. Occasional Paper. Marc Europe.

'Lessons in Leadership'. Paper by Super-Consultant Warren Bennis. *Bottom Line Personnel* Vol 17 No 3. 1 July 1996.

'Managing in an Enterprise Context'. A paper delivered by Dr D. Harper of Hallam University Business School, January 1994.

'Managing in Enterprise Contexts'. Ed. Bill Richardson. Pavic Publications, Sheffield Hallam University, 1993.

'Methodism Divided'. Published by Faber, 1968.

'Methodist Work in New Towns and New Areas.' Methodist Church

Home Mission Department, 1969.

'New City – Milton Keynes 1975'. Milton Keynes Development Corporation, p13.

'New Towns – The British Experience'. Published by Charles Knight for the Town and Country Planning Association, 1972, p 147.

'Now to Him'. Methodist Church Home Mission Report 115, 1971.

'Outreach in New Towns and Areas'. Report prepared by the Revd Francis C. Godfrey BSc. BD, the Revd Roy Gunstone BD, the Revd Michael Meech, and Mr Huw Rees Dip S Sc. for the Methodist Home Mission Department Report, April 1969. Reprinted February 1970.

'Population and Social Survey 1976'. Report published by the Skelmersdale New Town Development Corporation. Economic activity tabled – Part IV.

'Priorities'. Methodist Church Home Mission Report 120, 1976.

'Religion and Modernization'. Ed. Steve Bruce. Clarendon Press: Oxford, 1992. Paper: 'Secularization – The Orthodox Model' by Roy Wallis and Steve Bruce, p 19.

'Religion and Social Conflicts'. Olto Madun. Orbis: Maryknoll, 1982, p43.

'Religion and Society in Industrial England'. Longman, 1986.

'Secular City: New Jerusalem'. Report of a Conference on Planning for Mission, Bulletin No. 4 of the New Town Ministers Association.

'Shechem'. Handbook for the New Town Ministers Annual Conference. 21–24 April 1971.

'Stability and Strife: Great Britain – politics and government 1714–1760'. Arnold, 1977, p92.

'The Divided Society: Party Conflict in England 1694–1716'. Ed. Geoffrey Holmes and W. A. Speck. Arnold, 1967, p50.

'The Hidden Games of Organisations'. Translated by Arnold Pomerans. (Pantheon Books: New York, 1986).

'The Making of Ministry'. Report of Ministerial Training Policy Working Group, Methodist Council, 1996.

'The Making of Post-Christian Britain'. (Longman, 1981).

'The Testing of the Churches – 1932–1982'. (Epworth, 1982).

'The Works of John Wesley'. Vol 9. Ed. Rupert E Davies. (Abingdon Press).

(Evaluation of Questionnaire submitted by report to the second meeting of the Woughton Sub-committee on Monday 8th January 1979.)

(General Rules of the United Societies.)

(Gillies' Journal.)

(Group Processes. Ed. Clyde Hendrick. Sage Publications, 1987. Chapter 7: Influencing Process in Decision Making, p195.)

(Hansard. 1110. 5 April 1977.)

(Interview with the Revd David Robertson, Minister at Fishermead – 26 Talland Avenue, Fishermead.)

(Interview with the Revd Freda Beveridge, Anglican Deacon for Woolstones and Netherfield – 205 Beadlemead, Netherfield, MK6 4HU.)

(Interview with the Revd Hugh Cross, Ecumenical Moderator for Milton Keynes – 212 Bradwell Common Boulevard, Bradwell Common, MK13 8AB.)

(Interview with the Revd Steven Foster, Team Leader, Woughton Ecumenical Project – 47 Garraways, Coffee Hall, MK6 5DD.)

(Report of Joint Churches Working Party on Milton Keynes, 1970.)

(Market and Opinion Research International (MORI), for *The Times* and *Sunday Times*. Regular surveys.)

(Memorandum from the Ministers Fraternal, November 1967. 'The Purpose and Function of the Ecumenical Centre. Methodist Division of Home Mission Archive.)

(Memorandum of a Consultation between the Revd H. Sinclair Walker, member of staff responsible for New Towns at the Methodist Division of Home Mission and the Revd Chris Lee, Minister at Skelmersdale.)

(Memorandum of a conversation between Sinclair Walker, the Revd Victor Taylor, Superintendent Minister of Milton Keynes, and the Chairman of the District, 1 March 1971.)

(Memorandum of a private meeting between the Revd G. Sails, A. Kingsley Turner, V. Taylor and J. Harris, 4 December 1972.)

(Memorandum of the Skelmersdale New Town Commission, 10 March 1971, Home Mission Division Archive.)

(Memorandum of the Skelmersdale Methodist Commission on the New Town, 7 March 1973. Methodist Home Mission Division Archive.)

(Memorandum on the meeting of the Methodist New Town Commission on Skelmersdale, 3 March 1975. Methodist Home Mission Archive.)

(Memorandum on the Skelmersdale New Town Commission held at the Ecumenical Centre, Skelmersdale on Monday 1 March 1976. Home Mission Division Archive.)

(Memorandum on the Skelmersdale Commission, 8th March 1972. Methodist Home Mission Archive.)

(*Milton Keynes Report*. Published by the Information Unit, Milton Keynes Development Corporation as a newspaper, Summer 1978, p8.)

(Minutes of the meeting of Woughton Sub-committee, 17 May 1979.)

(Minutes of the Milton Keynes New Town Commission, called by the Methodist Church, 20 November 1969, Westminster.)

(Minutes of the Milton Keynes Commission, 19 November 1970.)

(Minutes of the Milton Keynes Methodist New Town Commission Meeting, 17 November 1971.)

(Minutes of the Woughton Ecumenical Sub-committee, 27 September 1978.)

(National Opinion Poll, published by NOP in 1982.)

(New Towns Act 1965. HM Stationery Office. Reprinted 1967.)

(Paper of the Notting Assembly of the Nationwide Initiative in Evangelism, held at the University of Nottingham, 1975.)

(Paper to the Annual Conference of the New Town Ministers Association, 1974.)

(Press Statement. Department of the Environment, April 1977.)

(Progress Report of the Skelmersdale Ecumenical Centre, 1972. Methodist Home Mission Division Archive.)

(Questionnaire of the Woughton Ecumenical Parish, May 1979.)

(Report to the Home Mission Division by the local Skelmersdale Fraternal of ministers advocating the opening of an ecumenical centre. Undated – approximately 1969.)

(Report of the Census of 1931 for England and Wales.)

(Report of the Evangelical Alliance New Towns Study Group: 'Evangelical strategy in the New Towns', published 1971 by the Evangelical Alliance.)

(Report of the Milton Keynes Circuit to the District Synod, May 1977.)

(Report of the Ministry of Housing and Local Government, 1960, p 96, Cmnd, 1435.)

(Report of the Skelmersdale Circuit to the Loughborough Consultation, 1975. Home Mission Division Archive.)

(Report on Basic Plan of Skelmersdale New Town, December 1964, p30.)

(Report on the New Town Ministers Association Annual Conference, 1973.)

(Report on The Skelmersdale United Congregation Questionnaire, 1977. Methodist Church Home Mission Division Archive.)

(Report to the Joint Ecumenical Council for Skelmersdale, 1975.

Methodist Home Mission Division Archive.)

(Reports on church life. Ecumenical Centre Publication, 1993.)

(Statement of Purpose, Aims and Objectives by the United Christian Congregation, December 1977. Methodist Division of Home Mission Archive.)

(Statistics from the Methodist Division of Education and Youth.)

(Wesley's Journal 9 May and 12 May 1739 and 15 February 1742.)

(Whitefield's Journal.)

Bibliography

Abbey, Charles J. and John H. Overton. *The English Church.*

Abraham, William. *The Logic of Evangelism.* Hodder and Stoughton, 1981.

Abraham-Williams, Gethin. *Steps along the way. The Course of Christian Unity 1967–1987 in Milton Keynes.* Milton Keynes Christian Council, 1987.

Anthony, Peter. *Managing Culture.* Open University Press, 1994, pp28,37.

Baker, Robin (Team Rector of Woughton) and Christopher Newton (Dean of Milton Keynes). *The Woughton Area and the Churches.* 3 January 1973.

Banks, R. A. *Drama and Theatre Arts.* London, 1985.

Beal, Patricia. *Growing Together in God's Family.* Celebration, 1983.

Beasley-Murray, Paul and Alan Wilkinson. *Turning the Tide. An Assessment of Baptist Church Growth in England.* The Bible Society, 1990.

Bebington, David. *Modern Christian Revivals.* Ed. Edith Blumhofer and Randall Bulmer, 1993. Chapter 2 – 'Revival and Enlightenment in 18th Century England' p30/31.

Beckett, Fran. *Called to Action.* Fount, 1989.

Bell, Bush, Fox, Goodey, Goulding. *Conducting Small-Scale Investigations in Educational Management.* Chaper 2 – 'Action Research', Cohen and Manion, p43. Published in association with Open University, 1984.

Beresford Hope, A. J. B. *Worship in the Church of England.* 1874. p17.

Berger, Peter L. *Making Sense of Modern Times. The Vision of Interpretive Sociology.* Ed. James Davison Hunter and Stephen C. Ainlay. Routledge and Kegan Paul, 1987.

Berger, Peter L. *The Social Reality of Religion*. Penguin, 1967, p131.

Bilton, Tony, Kevin Bonnett, Philip Jones, Michelle Stanworth, Ken Sheard and Andrew Webster. *Introductory Sociology*. (2nd Ed). Macmillan, 1882. (2nd Ed. 1987) p422.

Bird Matt. *Is Church Growth the Result of Methodology or the Work of God?* Supervisor Dr Martin Stringer.

Bird, Matt. *Leadership Training Manual*. Pioneer,1995.

Blaendulais. Ecumenical Centre Commission paper, 1969.

Bowmer, J. C. *Pastor and People*. Epworth Press, 1975, p191.

Brady, Steve and Harold Rowden. *For Such a Time as This*. Scripture Union, 1996.

Bready, J. Wesley. *England Before and After Wesley*. Hodder and Stoughton, May 1938.

Brierley, Peter. *Christian England*. Marc Europe, 1991.

Brierley, Peter. *Churchgoers in England*. Challenge 2000 and Christian Research.

Bromley, Eileen. *Christian Issues in the Gospels*. Stanley Thorne, 1991.

Brooke Taylor, G. Director of Social Development, Telford Development Corporation. Paper: 'Social Development'.

Brooke Taylor, G. Director of Social Development, Telford Development Corporation. Paper: 'New Towns: The British Experience'. Published by Town and Country Planning Association, 1972.

Brown, R. 1965. *Social Psychology*. New York: Free Press.

Brown, Richard. *Church and State in Modern Britain: A Political and Religious History*. Routledge, 1991.

Burnstein, E. and K. Sentis. *Attitude Polarization in Groups*. 1981

Byng, J. Torrington *Diaries*. Vol 111. p115.

Calver, Clive. 'Signs of Hope'. Article in the *Christian Herald*, 30 March 1991.

Calver, Clive. *Thinking Clearly About Truth*. Monarch Publications, 1995.

Carson. D. A. *Biblical Interpretation and the Church*. WEF, 1993.

Chadwick, O. *The Secularization of the European Mind in the 19th Century*. Cambridge University Press, 1975. p264.

Chambers, E. K. *The Medieval Stage*. Oxford, 1903, pp1-67.

Chandler, A. D. *Strategy and Structure*. MIT Press, 1962.

Child, J. *The Contribution of Organization Structure: Organizations as Systems*. Ed. Martin Lockett and Roger Spear. The Open University Press: Milton Keynes, 1980, p98.

Christopher, S. W. *Class Meetings in Relation to the Design and Success of Methodism.* Wesleyan Conference Office, 1873. p22.

Church of England. *Good News in our Times.* Church House, 1991.

Clarke, Philip A. *Being a Mission Church.* Cliff College, 1994.

Cohen and Manion. Ed. Judith Bell and others. *Conducting Small-Scale Investigations in Educational Management.* Chapter 2 – 'Action Research'. p41. Open University, 1984.

Cole, G. A. *Strategic Management.* DP Publications, 1994 pp 2, 10, 81, 137.

Cole, G. D. H. and Raymond Postgate. *The Common People* 1746-1946. Methuen, 1938. p16.

Cormack, Dr David. 'Leadership Styles, based on the Tannenbaum Schmidt Model'. From *Team Spirit.* Monarch Publications, 1987.

Cracknell, Kenneth. *Mission and Evangelism in Methodist Theological Inquiry and Education.* 1996

Cresswell, Peter and Ray Thomas. 'Employment and Population Balance'. A paper in *'New Towns: The British Experience'.* Published by Town and Country Planning Association, 1972.

Currie, Robert Alan Gilbert and Lee Horsley. *Churches and Church-Goers: Patterns of Church Growth in the British Isles since 1700.*

Currie, Robert. *Methodism Divided.* Faber, 1968.

Dallimore, A. *George Whitefield.* Vol. 1., Banner of Truth, 1970.

Davies. J. G. 'Church Growth: A Critique'. *International Review of Missions.* Vol 57. July 1968. pp291-197.

Davies, Rupert E. *Methodism.* Epworth Press, pp20/21.

Dawson, John. *Taking Our Cities For God.* Word, 1989.

Deal, T. and Kennedy A. *Corporate Cultures: The Rites and Rituals of Corporate Life.* 1982.

Defoe. ii 195. *From The Whig Supremacy. 1714-1760.* Basil Williams: Oxford (Clarendon) 1962 p126.

Dennington, Evelyn. (Member of Stevenage Development Corporation since 1950 and chairman since 1965) – 'New Towns for whom?' Paper in *New Towns, The British Experience.* Published by Charles Knight for the Town and Country Planning Association, 1972.

Digby, Ann and C. H. Feinstein. *New Directions in Economic and Social History.* 1989. p72.

Dixon, Patrick. *Out of the Ghetto and into the City.* Word, 1995.

Donavan, Vincent J. *Christianity Rediscovered.* SCM, 1986.

Durkheim, Emile. *The Elementary Forms of the Religious Life.* London, 1968.

Ecclestone, Giles. *The Parish Church.* Mowbray, 1988.

Edwards, M. L. *After Wesley 1791-1851.* Epworth Press,1935. pp 142-144; 163-171.

Egner, Malcolm. *Mission Impossible.* Scripture Union, 1990.

Eisenhart, M. A. 'The Ethnographic Research Tradition and Mathematics Education Research' in *Journal for Research in Mathematics Education,* Vol. 19, 1988 No 2 pp 99-114.

English, Donald. *Into the 21st Century.* Methodist Church Home Mission, 1995.

Evans, Andrew. Paper for Anglican delegation, 7 May 1993. Published by The Ecumenical Centre, Skelmersdale.

Everitt, A. *The Pattern of Rural Dissent in the Nineteenth Century.* Leicester University Press, 1972.

Forde, N. *Theatrecraft.* London, 1986.

Forster, Chris. *Planting For A Harvest.* Challenge 2000, 1995.

Frost, Rob. *Breaking Bread.* Kingsway, 1988.

Frost, Rob. Ph.D Thesis 'New Towns'. 1995

Gallup, George. *The International Public Opinion Polls – Great Britain 1937-75. 1976.*

Gay, J. D. *The Geography of Religion in England.* Duckworth, 1971. pp69ff.

Georgiou, George. *Attitude to Local Mission.* Bible Society, 1994.

Gibbs, Eddie. *I Believe in Church Growth.* Hodder & Stoughton, 1981.

Gilbert, Alan D. *The Making of Post-Christian Britain. A history of the secularization of modern society.* Longman, 1981.

Giles, Kevin. *What on Earth is the Church?* SPCK, 1995.

Gill, Robin. *Beyond Decline: A Challenge to the Churches.* SCM Press, 1988.

Glasner, P. *The Sociology of Secularization.* Routledge and Kegan Paul, 1977 p7.

Gollancz, Victor. *Mass-Observation, Puzzled People: A Study in Popular Attitudes to Religion. Ethics, Progress and Politics in a London Borough.* London, 1947.

Gowland, D. A. *Methodist Secession.* Manchester University Press, 1979. p1.

Green, V. H. H. *The Young Mr Wesley. D. D.* Edward Arnold, 1961. p7.

Groome, Colin. *Right Up Your Street.* Christian Focus Publications, 1993.

Gumbel, Nicky. *Alpha Manual.* HTB Publications.

Haigh, C. *Reformation and Resistance in Tudor Lancashire.* Cambridge

University Press, 1975. Chapter 2.

Halevy, E. *A History of the English People in 1815*. Penguin Books, 1938. p21.

Halsey, A. H. *Change in British Society*. Opus.

Halsey, A. H. *Educational Priority. Vol. 1. EPA Problems and Policies*. HMS0, 1972.

Hammond, J. L and B. *The Town Labourer*, 1760-1832 Vol 1. Guild Books. 1949. p18.

Hammond, J. L. and B. op.cit. Vol 2, pp 94-95.

Hanchey, Howard. *Church Growth and the Power of Evangelism*. Cowley, 1990.

Handy, Charles. *The Gods of Management*. Century Business, 1991 edition.

Harding, Joe A. & Ralph W. Mohney. *Vision 2000. Discipleship Resources*. 1991

Harper, Dr David. 'Going for New Growth in a Christian Setting'. Paper submitted for 'Managing in an Enterprise Context' conference, University of Hallam Business School, January 1994. York.

Harris, Jeffrey. *Our Calling to Fulfil*. Methodist Church Home Mission Division, 1986.

Harrison, R. *Organisation Culture and Quality of Service*. AMED, 1987.

Heathcote, D. *Drama as a Learning Medium*. Ed B. J. Wagner. London, 1979.

Hill, C. *Economic Problems of the Church*. Panther, 1971. p351.

Hobsbawm, E. J. *Industry and Empire*. Penguin Books, 1968. pp21,86.

Hoggart, Richard. *The Uses of Literacy*.

Hollenweger, Walter J. Guest Editorial in the *International Review of Missions*. Vol 57. July 1968. pp271-277.

Hopenell, J. F. *Congregation: Stories and Structures*. SCM, 1987.

Hornbrook, D. *Education and Dramatic Art*. Oxford, 1989.

Horsley, Graham. *One Plus One*. Methodist Church Home Mission Division, 1992.

Horsley, Graham. *Planting New Congregations*. Methodist Church Home Mission Division, 1994.

Hughes-Smith, Christopher. 'Belonging to a Multi-Cultural Church'. Occasional paper for the Methodist Division of Home Mission. Undated.

Humphreys, A. R. *The Augustan World*. University Paperbacks (Methuen), 1954 p145.

Hunter, George G. *The Contagious Congregation*. Abingdon, 1979.

Hunter, George G. *To Spread the Power*. Abingdon, 1987.

Jameson, Frederic. *Postmodernism: Or: The Cultural Logic of Late Capitalism*. Verso, 1991.

John, Matthew P. 'Evangelism and the Growth of the Church'. *International Review of Missions*. Vol 57. July 1968. pp278-283.

Johnstone, Patrick. *Operation World*. OM, 1993.

Jones, D. H. R. *Planning for Mission: A Study in Church Decision Making in New Towns*. New Town Ministers Association.

Jones, Richard. *Skelmersdale Ecumenical Centre – a History and Evaluation*. Methodist Division of Home Mission Archive, May 1978.

Jordan, Bishop O. P. 'Numerical Growth – An Adequate Criterion of Mission?' *International Review of Missions* Vol 57, July 1968. pp284-290.

Kane. J. Herbert. *The Christian World Mission: Today and Tomorrow*. Baker Book House: USA, 1981.

Karup, Helen. 'Conventional Religion and Common Religion in Leeds'. Interview Schedule: Basic frequencies by question, Leeds. University of Leeds Department of Sociology, Religious Research Paper 12, 1982.

Kelly, J. N. D. *Early Christian Doctrines*. A & C Black, 1968.

Kendrick, Graham. *Ten Worshipping Churches*. MARC, 1983.

Kessler, Jr. J. B. A. 'Hindrances to Church Growth'. *International Review of Missions*. Vol 57, July 1968. pp298-303.

Lamont, G. and R. *Drama Toolkit*. Buckingham, 1993.

Leavitt, Harold, William Dill, Henry Eyring. *The Organizational World: A Systematic View of Managers and Management*. Harcourt Brace Jovanovich, 1973.

Lecky, William. *A History of England in the Eighteenth Century*. Vol 2. New York, 1887. p595.

Lee, Chris. Submission to the Home Mission Division,1970. Home Mission Archive.

Little, Stephen. Paper submitted to the Milton Keynes New Town Commission in July 1884. Social Responsibility Vicar (Anglican) for Milton Keynes.

Lockett, Martin and Roger Spear. *Organizations as Systems*. The Open University Press, 1980. Paper by L. W. Stern titled 'Potential Conflict Management Mechanisms'.

Lyon, David. *The Steeple's Shadow*. SPCK, 1985.

Macdonald, A., S. Stickley and P. Hawthorn. *Street Theatre*. Minstrel, 1991.

Martin, Charles. *Schools Now*.

Martin, David. 'Age and Sex Variations of Church Attenders'. In *Nationwide Initiative in Evangelism* Ed Peter Brierley.

Mathias, P. *The First Industrial Nation*. Methuen, 1969. p186.

Mathison, John (Ed.) *Every Member in Ministry*. Discipleship Resources 1988.

McClatchey, D. *Oxfordshire Clergy 1771-1869*. Oxford University Press,1960. Chs 2-5.HMGB 11, pp 13ff, 49-55.

McGavran, Donald A. 'Church Growth Strategy Continued'. *International Review of Missions*. Vol 57, July 1968. pp335-343.

McGuire, Meredith B. *Religion: The Social Context*. Wadsworth Publishing, 1991 p 150.

Miles, Christine & Catherine Butcher. *On Fire Mission Strategy Manual*. CPO.

Mintzberg, H. and J. B. Quinn. *The Entrepreneurial Organization*. p 607. 1991.

Mintzberg, H. 'Planning on the Left Side, Managing in the Right'. *Harvard Business Review*, July 1976.

Montgomery, Jim. *7 Million Churches to Go. Dawn 2000*. Highland, 1990.

Moore. *The Life of Mrs Mary Fletcher*. p126.

Munsey Turner, John. *Conflict and Reconciliation: Studies in Methodism and Ecumenism in England 1740-1982*.

Munson, James. *The Nonconformists. In Search of a Lost Culture*. SPCK, 1991. pp 302-305.

Naisbitt, John. *Megatrends*. 1982.

Newlands, George. *The Church of God*. Marshall Morgan & Scott, 1984.

Oakland, John. *British Civilisation*. Routledge, 1991. p224.

Odgers, Nicholas. *The Methodist Class Meeting*. Kent and Co. p29. (undated).

Osborn, Frederic J. and Arnold Whittick. *New Towns – Their Origins, Achievements and Progress*. Leonard Hill, 1963, 1969, 1977.

Ostling, Richard N. 'Those Mainline Blues'. *Time Magazine*, May 1989.

Overton, John Henry. *Evangelical Revival in the Eighteenth Century*. Longman, Green and Company,1886.

Patrick, Bruce. *Multiplication of Congregations*. Baptist Union of New

Zealand, 1989.

Pitt, Gillian. (Resident in Crawley new town for fifteen years, tutor in social science at Brighton Polytechnic.) 'A Consumer's View'. Paper in *New Towns: The British Experience*. Town and Country Planning Association, 1972.

Rack, Henry D. 'The Future of John Wesley's Methodism' in *Ecumenical Studies in History*. Ed. A. M. Allchin, Martin E. Marty, T. H. L. Parker., 1964.

Richardson, Bill, Anthea Gregory and Sara Turton. *Managing In Enterprise Contexts*. Ed. Bill Richardson. 'Towards a profile of a visionary leader'. PAVIC Publications, Sheffield Hallam University, 1993 pp9-11.

Roof, Wade. and William McKinney. *American Mainline Religion.*

Rothwell, Roy and Walter Zegveld. *Innovation and the Small and Medium Sized Firm.* Frances Pinter, 1982, p96.

Rupp, G. *Religion in England 1688-1791*, Clarendon Press, 1986.

Rupp, George, A. R. and E. G. *A History of the Methodist Church in Great Britain*, Vol 3. Epworth, 1983.

Sands, Nigel. *The Skelmersdale Story*. Published by the Parish Church in 1970.

Schaffer, Frank. *The New Town Story*. Macgibbon and Kee, 1970. p242.

Schein, E.H. *Organizational Culture and Leadership.* Jossey-Bass: USA, 1985.

Schmidt, Martin. *John Wesley, A Theological Biography.* Vol. 1 (1703-1738). Epworth Press, 1962. p. 232.

Schon, D. A. 'Champions for Radical New Inventions'. *Harvard Business Review* March/April 1965. pp77-86.

Selby, Peter. *Belonging.* SPCK, 1991.

Sharp, Clifford & Noel. *Meltdown.* Nimbus, 1996.

Sheane, Derek. *Beyond Bureaucracy.* Management Research, 1976.

Sherif, M. 'Experiments in Group Conflict'. *Scientific American,* CXCV, 1956. 54-58.

Simon, John S. *John Wesley, The Last Phase.* Epworth Press, 1934. p 211.

Socket, Barbara. *A Stone is Cast.* Birkenhead. pp23.

Southey, Robert. *The Life of John Wesley.* Hutchinson, 1820. p12.

Speck, William Arthur. *Stability and Strife.* Edward Arnold, 1977. p111.

Spring Harvest. *Dancing in the Dark?* Lynx, 1994.

Stevenson, John. *Popular Disturbances in England. 1700-1870.* Longman, 1979. p32.

Swift, Dean. 'Project for the Advancement of Religion'. 1709. Swift's *Works* viii 105.

Sylvester, J. 'The Church and the Geographer'. Liverpool *Essays in Geography*. Ed R. W. Steel and R. Lawton. Longman, 1967.

Taylor, Victor. Background information of planning development as it affects the churches. Personal statement, September 1972.

Thompson Brake, George. *Policy and Politics in British Methodism 1932-82*. Edsall, 1984. p697.

Trinder, B. *The Industrial Revolution in Shropshire*. Phillimore, 1973. p297.

Trinity Annual Conference. *Directions for the Fifth Quadrennium*. Methodist Church in Singapore, 1996.

Trinity Annual Conference. *Evangelising into the Next Century*. Methodist Church in Singapore, 1996.

Turner, John Munsey. *Conflict and Reconciliation*. 1922.

Tuperman, Wesley. *Life of Charles Wesley*. ii (1841). 391.

Vincent, John. *OK, Let's be Methodists*. Epworth Press, 1984.

Walker, Sinclair. Methodist Home Mission Department Annual Report 113. 1967/8.

Wallis, Roy and Steve Bruce. *Religion and Modernization*. Ed. Steve Bruce. Clarendon Press, 1992. 'Secularization – The Orthodox Model', p 42.

Walsh, J. D. *The Planting of Methodism in British Society*. WMHS Selly Oak Conference, 1975.

Ward, J. T. *The Age of Change. 1770-1870. Documents in Social History*. Black, 1975.

Ward, W. R. HMGB 11, p 53

Ward, W. R. HMGB 11 pp 54-55.

Ward, W. R. 'The Cost of Establishment: Church Buildings in Manchester'. *Studies in Church History*. Vol 111 Ed. G.J. Cuming. Leiden, 1966. pp 277-289.

Warner, Rob. *Twenty-first Century Church*. Hodder and Stoughton, 1993.

Watts, Murray. *Christianity and the Theatre*. The Handsel Press, 1986.

Wearmouth, R.F. *Methodism and the Working Class in the Eighteenth Century*. Epworth Press, 1945. p184. From Report on Act for Building Churches, 1821.

Wearmouth, R.F. *Methodism and Working Class Movements 1800-1850*. Epworth Press, 1937. pp 16-19.

Webb, S. and B. *History of Liquor Licensing*. pp17.18.

Wesley, John. *Letters*. Volume 1. p 289.

Wickham, E. R. *Church and People in an Industrial City*. Lutterworth Press, 1957. p80.

Wilkes, John. *United Kingdom: A Modern Social, Economic and Political History of Britain*. Cambridge University Press, 1984. p123.

Williams, Michael E. 'Society Today'. Based on a series from *New Society*. Macmillan, 1986. p155.

Williamson, Roy. *For Such A Time As This*. Darton Longman & Todd, 1996.

Wilson, B. *Religion in a Secular Society*. C. A. Watts and Co, 1966.

Wilson, Sir Hugh. Skelmersdale New Town-Planning Proposals D.C. 1964.

Wilson, W. Gilbert. *The Faith of an Anglican*. Fount, 1980.

Woodman, John. *The Wave of God – AD 2000*. 1995.